Flora, Fauna, & Faith

Autumn Devotionals Inspired by God's Creation

Flora, Fauna, & Faith

Autumn Devotionals Inspired by God's Creation

McGahan

Flora, Fauna, & Faith: Autumn Devotionals Inspired by God's Creation

Rooted & Flourishing *Devotional Series*

Copyright © 2022 by Andrea L. Robinson

MCGAHAN PUBLISHING HOUSE | LYNCHBURG, TENNESSEE

www.mphbooks.com

Requests for information should be sent to:

info@mphbooks.com

Cover Design by Marynn Spurlock

Photos & Graphics by Kaleigh Madison LLC

ISBN 978-1-951252-20-5

*To my mom, Debra, whose love of nature
and family inspired my own*

Contents

Acknowledgements

So many loved ones, friends, and colleagues contributed to this collection of devotionals in one way or another. I'm eternally thankful for the support system with which God has blessed me. First and foremost, I would like to thank my entire family for allowing me to share intimate details and embarrassing moments of our lives together. Thanks especially to my mom, Debra Kulaw, who played an integral part in the development of this book. From start to finish, your devotional ideas, gardening facts, constructive feedback, and family memories kept me inspired and motivated. For my husband, Wesley, who not only helped with household chores and kid duties while I wrote, but proofread every single devotional in the volume, your constant support and calming presence sustain me like nothing else. I would be remiss also not to thank my boys, Asher and Abel, who perennially endure the spotlight as sermon illustrations and devotional lessons.

Thank you to my beta readers Lynn Ferrell, Kim Walker, Laura Burke, Rachel Moore and Amy Kodra. Each of you provided unique feedback that made my writing better than before. To my long-time friends Tom Buckle, Lisa Buckle and Doug Sittason, who helped with beta reading and also served as sounding boards and dialogue partners for devo ideas, you'll never know how much it means to have friends who have stood by my side to through the

Acknowledgements

highest and lowest points of my life. Celebrating this accomplishment is even more meaningful because you are celebrating with me. To my pastors, Spencer and Ellen Beach, thank you for not only allowing me to divide my time between ministry and academics, but for championing my research and writing pursuits. For Caleb Poston and McGahan Publishing House, I want to express sincere gratitude. I'm honored that you have faith enough in my work not only to publish a book of devotionals, but to contract four volumes. I value your thoughtful responses and ongoing dialogue, which has taken my own ideas to the next level. Finally, thank you to Jesus, my Lord and Friend. I pray that my own imperfect efforts honor you and edify your people.

Introduction & Instructions

Hello friends,

You will get to know me well over the next weeks and months, but I'd like to introduce myself before we begin. I am a wife, mom, pastor, scholar, adventurer, fitness fanatic, animal lover, and avid gardener. I'm far from perfect, but I love Jesus, I love to learn, and I seize every day with joy. Despite my qualifications as a scholar, I'm irresponsible, impulsive, and sometimes obnoxious. Nonetheless, God allows me to serve Him in ways that astound me.

In January 2020 as I was fasting, I felt God compelling me to write a series of devotions inspired by nature. Although I normally focus more on academic writing, I was excited about the prospect of writing devotionals. I simply wasn't sure when I would have time to write them. As a pastor, wife, and mom of two boys, my schedule didn't exactly provide large blocks of writing time. Unbeknownst to me, God was already orchestrating the circumstances under which I would be writing devotionals on a daily basis.

As we now know, 2020 was the year in which we encountered the coronavirus, a quarantine, and an unprecedented degree of isolation. In an effort to encourage our church family, our church staff decided to produce daily devotionals, and I lead the project. Initially, I didn't make the connection between the devotionals God was calling me to write and the devotionals I was writing for our church. As time passed, however, I realized that God was helping me sow the seeds of my devotional project.

You now hold in your hands the first fruits of my labor of love. *Fall* is the first of four volumes, each of which corresponds to a different season of the year. As you read devotions that reflect the ebb and flow of the natural world, as well as the seasons in my own life, I pray you'll be encouraged, inspired, and challenged. I hope that some of the devos make you laugh and some of them make you cry. I expect you'll even learn a few things about God's creation. Most of all, I pray that you become more deeply rooted in God's presence, grow in your faith, and flourish in your life's journey.

Before you begin, allow me to offer a few suggestions. Each day, I've provided a devotional, a brief prayer, and a prompt for further reflection and meditation. I hope you will allow the prayer and reflection to serve as a launching point for further introspection and dialogue with the Father. In some instances, I've recommended a passage of Scripture for further reading, and in those cases a QR code has been provided for convenient access to the chapters or verses. For all Scripture passages cited in the devotionals, I've used the New Living Translation with the exception of verses I translated myself.

At the end of each devotional, I've included blank space for journaling. I sometimes offer journaling prompts, but the space is primarily for you to record spiritual insights, life lessons, and personal thoughts. As you pray, meditate, and journal, take time to listen for the still, small voice of God. Give him permission to uproot any weeds in the garden of your heart, create fertile soil for new growth, and plant the seeds of his will. — Andrea

Be sure to connect with me at **www.AndreaLeighRobinson.org** and on social media. I have additional content and interactive opportunities waiting for you!

Day 1
For Everything a Season

Life flows in seasons, and summer fades into fall. If you are like me, the end of summer feels bittersweet. As the temperature cools and the leaves turn brown, I'm sad because winter is coming soon. At the same time, I look forward to relief from scorching temperatures and oppressive humidity.

Just as the heat of summer is replaced by cool fall breezes, seasons of our life change with the passage of time. The author of Ecclesiastes describes the continuous changes in the current of life.

For everything there is a season,
a time for every activity under heaven.
A time to be born and a time to die.
A time to plant and a time to harvest.
A time to kill and a time to heal.
A time to tear down and a time to build up.
A time to cry and a time to laugh.
A time to grieve and a time to dance.
Ecclesiastes 3:1–4

Some seasons of life are characterized by celebration and some by mourning. Some seasons are peaceful, and some are chaotic. Some seasons are devoted to toil, while others are restful and refreshing.

I've written these devotionals to reflect seasons in the natural world, but also to reflect the ebbs and flows of life. Through acknowledging the dynamic nature of our existence, we can be more content in the present and better prepare for the future. Although we are often taken by surprise when our lives change, God isn't. Our Father watches over us every single day, in every season (Psalm 139:15–16). He clears the path before us, establishes our steps, and protects us from harm (Psalm 37:23–40). If you are in a difficult season right now, remember that it won't last forever. If you are in a season of rest, take the time to build upon your foundation in Christ, grow stronger, and prepare for whatever might come next.

Over the next days, weeks, and months, you and I will talk about making the most of every season. We'll allow God to speak through the natural world and seek his wisdom through creation. In tandem with Scripture, God offers powerful yet practical lessons for our lives. Together, we will talk about overcoming trials, fostering gratitude, cultivating holistic health, developing healthy relationships, and much more.

Just remember that no matter what season you are in, God has fresh mercies every day. The closer we draw to his presence, the greater access we have to his blessings. In his presence, we find an abundance of joy, peace, love, and everything else we need for today and every day.

Lord, thank you for guiding me through the seasons of life and for offering fresh mercies in each. Help me to fix my eyes on you so that I recognize every blessing you send. Give me the endurance to make the most of every season and every opportunity that you place before me. Help me to grow in perseverance and fortitude so that I remain faithful even during the difficult seasons of life. Show me what you would have me learn in every stage. Guide me as I seek to serve you faithfully and spread your love to others. In Jesus' name, Amen.

Personal Reflection

Prayerfully meditate on your current season of life. Write down as many blessings as you can think of and thank God for each one.

- Blessed to have more time to sit & be still w/ The Holy One
- Blessed to have a time to do life with my daughter Alyssa
- Blessed in my Relationships with Alyssa, Andy & Zach
- Blessed to be a Nonna
- Blessed in my desire to dive deeper in knowledge & understanding of the Word.
- Blessed to work for teachers
- Blessed that my home will be paid off before Retiring.
- Blessed with Health
- Blessed in Relationship with my Mom

Day 2
Worst Gardening Year Ever

As the 2021 gardening season drew to a close for the year, I felt a powerful sense of relief. Most growing seasons in my home state of Alabama are filled with sunny days and lush growth. But not the spring and summer of 2021, which was roughly 120 days of toil and frustration for me. I'll tell you more about it in the days to come, but let me offer a quick preview. First, we received unprecedented and excessive levels of rainfall, which facilitated the development of a scaly blight and the invasion of armyworms in my garden. To make matters worse, a large family of rabbits shacked up in my yard, which was kind of cute until they started eating every plant that the blight and armyworms didn't kill. The only thing that kept me from giving up was the fact that my yard would have looked like a horror scene if I hadn't taken action to mediate the damage. So, I continued to toil.

Whereas gardening usually brings me joy and refreshing, I felt frustrated and at times even repulsed. So, as I often do, I asked myself, "What can I learn?" I firmly believe that frustrations and failures can be redeemed by listening for God's wisdom and guidance.

As I listened for God's voice, He reminded me of another season of my life during which I had experienced feelings of frustration, failure, and devastation. For various reasons, I had resigned from a ministry position. I felt like God had abandoned me, and I wondered if I would ever return to ministry. But rather than abandoning me, God was simply taking me in a new direction and into a new season of life. Just because I went through one hard season didn't mean that I was going to quit forever. In fact, the shift propelled me into a PhD program, which led to massive personal, professional, and spiritual growth.

In Scripture, God never promises that our lives will be easy or free from pain. In fact, Jesus explicitly tells us that "In this world you will have trouble" (John 16:33). But we also have hope, through Jesus, that our God won't allow us to suffer forever. In fact, Peter says that Jesus will personally restore us: "In his kindness God called you to share in his eternal glory by means of Christ Jesus. So, after you have suffered a little while, he will restore, support, and strengthen you, and he will place you on a firm foundation ..." (1 Peter 5:10).

As Peter comforts us with the promise of restoration, he also reminds us of the scope and magnitude of God's power. You may feel like your affliction is more than you can handle, but Jesus will provide the strength you need. He hasn't abandoned us or forgotten us, but rather, walks with us through our trials and empowers us to emerge stronger than before.

By the fall of 2021, I had learned a lot of gardening lessons. The learning process wasn't very fun, but I'm better equipped now to deal with future obstacles and dilemmas. I don't always take joy in the challenges, but I do love an opportunity to learn!

Lord, thank you for strengthening, supporting, and restoring me in your perfect timing. Help me to trust in your power and sovereignty. Help me to focus upon your love and grace rather than fixate on my problems. Show me what I can learn from every trial or difficulty I face, whether big or small. In Jesus' name, Amen.

Personal Reflection

If God immediately rescued us from every trial, we would miss out on valuable life lessons and growth opportunities. What can you learn from your current trials and problems? What lessons has God taught you through past trials, for which you can now give thanks? What can you do to better equip yourself to successfully navigate trials in the future?

_____

_____

_____

_____

_____

_____

_____

_____

_____

_____

_____

_____

_____

Day 3
Armyworms

The summer of 2021 brought a plague of biblical proportions. Within the span of a week, the entirety of north Alabama was covered in armyworms, or at least it seemed that way to me. Individually, they can't do much damage, but collectively, they can demolish any vegetation in proximity. Their attack is two-pronged. First, they eat grass and leaves above the ground. Then, they burrow under the soil, eating tender roots as they prepare to pupate. They can strip your entire yard within a couple of days. Any vegetation that does remain will be dead and brown due to root damage.

Lest you've never experienced an armyworm invasion, and I hope you haven't, allow me to paint a portrait of the invasion. My yard was so carpeted in worms that I couldn't walk across the grass without stepping on a smattering of them. The pests even made their way onto non-green spaces, inching their way onto my patio, creeping onto our driveway, and dribbling over the curb.

When I initially saw the armyworms, my first response was to cringe in horror, run inside, and shut the door. My second response was to declare war. I simply couldn't leave my garden to the mercy of the ravaging horde. I immediately called our beleaguered pest-control technician, who employed the only weapon at our disposal—pesticide. As I try to avoid using harmful chemicals in my garden, I was relieved to learn that the armyworm spray was non-toxic. It wouldn't harm humans or beneficial insects that I want to keep in my garden.

Despite my aversion to pesticides, I never considered allowing the armyworms to stay. Seeking to develop a truce with the horde of worms would be utterly ridiculous. In a similar manner, the authors of Scripture repeatedly warn us not to compromise with the Enemy. Jesus teaches, "Anyone who isn't with me opposes me, and anyone who isn't working with me is actually working against me," (Matthew 12:30). Living for Christ while cooperating with the Enemy simply isn't possible. Although we should show love and grace to all people, we can't allow ourselves to make a truce with sin.

We may feel like we have our compromised situation in hand, but in truth, we are actually exhibiting a lack of self-control, and according to Solomon, "A person without self-control is like a city with broken-down walls," (Proverbs 25:28). When we fail to stand decisively with God against the enemy, we become like a defenseless city—exposed to attack and vulnerable to the weapons of the Enemy. Compromise is akin to tearing down the very walls God has erected for our protection. Just as I had to employ defensive measures to guard against an invading force of worms, we must maintain the strength of our spiritual lines of defense.

When we resolutely ally with our father, he both protects and blesses us. We can confidently claim the promises Moses spoke to the nation of Israel as they prepared to enter the Promised Land:

You will experience all these blessings if you obey
the Lord your God:
Your towns and your fields
will be blessed.
Your children and your crops
will be blessed.
The offspring of your herds and flocks
will be blessed.

Your fruit baskets and breadboards
will be blessed.
Wherever you go and whatever you do,
you will be blessed.
"The Lord will conquer your enemies when they at-
tack you. They will attack you from
one direction, but they will scatter from you in
seven!
Deuteronomy 28:2–7

God will protect and bless us when we obediently remain within the boundaries he has created. He doesn't promise that our lives will be perfect or easy, but he does promise blessing, protection and victory! Let's fortify our hearts, stand our ground, and fight for our faith. The Enemy can send his army of nasty little worms, but we'll be ready for battle.

Heavenly Father, thank you for being my protector and provider. Thank you for placing boundaries in my life to keep me safe. Forgive me for compromising my faith with thoughts, words, and behaviors that dishonor you. I confess that I have often made myself vulnerable to the schemes of the Enemy. Equip me to boldly live out my faith and humbly submit to your guidance. Give me the self-discipline to live in holiness and obedience. Thank you for showering me with blessings on a daily basis, even when I don't deserve your grace. In Jesus' Name, Amen.

Personal Reflection

Prayerfully ask God to show you any areas of your life in which you are compromising your faith. List them below, then ask God to show you how each one makes you vulnerable to the schemes of the Enemy. Beside each, write down why you want to remove or replace the area of compromise with something that fortifies your faith.

_____

_____

_____

_____

_____

_____

_____

_____

_____

_____

_____

_____

_____

_____

_____

_____

Day 4
The Pinching Beetle

My younger sister Ginger and I are about four years apart. I have one particularly vivid memory of an incident from when we were roughly two and six years old. She was in the phase during which any and all objects go into the mouth. It's a completely natural way that kids explore the world and satisfy curiosity. Unfortunately, the phase is also accompanied by a lack of good judgment.

On the day in question, Ginger and I were playing outside when she discovered a rather large and interesting type of bug. I watched in horror as Ginger deposited the bug headfirst into her mouth too quickly for me to intervene. Unfortunately, this bug was a stag beetle, also known as a pinching beetle. If you've never seen one, a pinching beetle has large, serrated mandibles that extend from its head like antlers. As expected, the beetle clamped down on Ginger's tongue. I can still see her standing there, red-faced and wailing as only a two-year-old can with the beetle clamped onto her tongue. I didn't know what to do, so I ran for backup and found Mom. I don't really remember what happened after that, but suffice to say that the beetle was removed from Ginger's tongue. It was quite the harrowing experience, but also a hilarious memory.

So, what is the moral of the story? Even as adults, we love to sample the world around us. We enjoy new experiences, new places, new media, new food. We love to explore everything the world has to offer, but like that beetle, sometimes what the world has to offer is harmful. Sometimes, a new experience or opportunity might not be damaging, it simply isn't God's will for us.

What if, instead of dashing from day to day and experience to experience, we sought guidance and direction first? Although we can and should learn from bad experiences, God often provides a way to bypass trials entirely. In Romans, Paul describes how we can avoid the pitfalls of worldly temptations. "Don't copy the behavior and customs of this world, but let God transform you into a new person by changing the way you think. Then you will learn to know God's will for you, which is good and pleasing and perfect," (Romans 12:2).

When we saturate our thinking in God's Word and pray diligently, we will learn to walk in the good plans of God. Because our thinking is aligned with His will, we will be able to discern what is pleasing to Him and what is harmful to ourselves. Rather than a pinching beetle to the tongue, we will be able to "taste and see that the Lord is good" (Psalm 34:8).

Lord, thank you for providing me with the discernment to avoid pitfalls and walk in your will. Help me continue to grow in discernment and pray diligently. Give me a desire to study your Word so that my thinking is continually transformed and aligned with your will for my life. Help me be sensitive to the guidance of the Holy Spirit and to live in obedience. Thank you for your good, pleasing, and perfect will for my life. In Jesus' name, Amen.

Personal Reflection

Prayerfully determine one step you can take in order to transform your thinking to a greater degree. You might resolve to pray or study more regularly. Perhaps you need to make a habit of praying and asking for God's guidance throughout your day. You may need to align your thought patterns with the truth of God's word. Ask the Holy Spirit to guide you as you seek to live out the perfect will of God for your life.

_____

_____

_____

_____

_____

_____

_____

_____

_____

_____

_____

_____

Day 5

Peppers, Peppers, and More Peppers!

The summer of 2021 was a horrible gardening year with one exception: peppers. My pepper crop abounded. Bell peppers, jalapenos, poblanos—I had more peppers than I knew what to do with. Even though Wesley, Asher, and Abel didn't really like to eat peppers, I started adding them to our meals anyway. I chopped the peppers into tiny pieces, snuck them into casseroles, and hoped that no one would notice. Eventually though, Wesley and the boys confessed that, not only were they aware of the peppers, but they were also enjoying them as well. I rejoiced at their approval and began to put peppers in everything. I used peppers so much that Wesley quipped that we would soon have jalapeno ice cream.

Yesterday, we discussed evaluating new experiences in the light of Scripture and proceeding prayerfully. But even when we sense God's blessing upon a new opportunity, we are often hesitant to move forward. Trying something new or different from your norm can be intimidating. When we step out of our comfort zone, we can feel vulnerable and afraid. God, however, delights in new beginnings. The Psalmist expresses this principle repeatedly. In Psalm 40:3, he says, "[God] has given me a new song to sing, a hymn of praise to our God. Many will see what he has done and be amazed. They will put their trust in the Lord."

When we follow the guidance of the Lord, he often leads us to new opportunities and new seasons of life. In our initial season of salvation, he gives us a new song, and then he continues to challenge and refine us on a daily basis. What if we stepped out of our comfort zone and stepped into each new challenge? As Psalm 40:3 says, many will see the amazing works of the Lord and put their trust in him. Trying new things doesn't benefit you alone but blesses others in ways of which you may not even be aware. Instead of tiny bits of pepper, grab fresh mercies and new experiences, and let them spice up your faith!

Lord, thank you for placing a new song in my heart, and thank you for the new opportunities you provide each day. Thank you for challenging me and helping me grow. Help me to recognize fresh occasions for personal growth and for ministry. I pray that as I step out of my comfort zone, other people would be blessed by placing faith in God. Help me be bold and unafraid as I serve you. In Jesus' name, Amen.

Personal Reflection

Meditate on potential growth opportunities that God may be placing before you. Make an effort to try something new, even if you feel vulnerable or afraid. Remember that your step of faith encourages others to trust in the Lord!

_____

_____

_____

_____

_____

_____

Day 5

Day 6
Rascally Rabbits

Humans aren't the only creatures that enjoy eating peppers. Rabbits also love them, or at least, the rabbits that live in my yard. Most rabbits tend to avoid peppers, and pepper spray can even be used on plants to keep pests away. But once my rabbits had a taste for peppers, they couldn't get enough. Short of killing the rabbits, I tried every method of repelling them known to humankind. Even my two dogs couldn't keep the rabbits out of the yard.

My only recourse was to dig the pepper plants up, put them in large pots, and move them to my patio. Once there, my pepper plants were finally in an environment in which they could thrive. Their location was also convenient for me. Any time I needed peppers for cooking, I could step right out the back door to grab a few. Thankfully, the rabbits weren't brazen enough to forage at my back door.

God often uses difficult or uncomfortable circumstances as a catalyst for change in our lives. Prior to his conversion, the Apostle Paul had been an exceptional and devout Jewish rabbi. Upon receiving the salvation of Christ, Paul began traveling from city to city passionately sharing the Good News with both Jews and Gentiles. Sadly, Paul's own people routinely responded to him with abhorrence and violence. I can't imagine how Paul would have felt upon sharing his wonderful news with the people he had loved and served his whole life, only to be scorned and mocked.

Day 6

Acts 18 describes the turning point in Paul's ministry. Luke describes how the Jewish people of Corinth opposed and insulted Paul. Done with their ridicule, Paul "shook the dust from his clothes and said, 'Your blood is upon your own heads—I am innocent. From now on I will go preach to the Gentiles,'" (Acts 18:6). Through Paul's pain, God guided the apostle to his ultimate calling—ministry to the gentiles.

Just a few days ago we discussed persevering through difficult seasons and learning from them, but that doesn't mean that we have to stay in trial indefinitely. Sometimes what God is trying to teach us is that we need to take action and make a change. Perhaps you need an outward change, like a change of location. Or perhaps you need to change the type of ministry in which you are involved, like Paul. Most often though, internal change brings the most significant and lasting growth in our lives. Your discomfort could be the result of an unresolved trauma, an unforgiven offense, a wrong pattern of thinking, or a harmful behavior. Before you make any external changes in hopes that your problems will go away, be sure to look inward.

Lord, thank you for using even the painful and uncomfortable areas of my life to bring growth. Help me become more aware of opportunities for positive change in my life. Guide me as I evaluate my thoughts and emotions so that I can move toward lasting health. Give me the courage to make changes where they are needed. Give me the strength to refrain from taking steps that will only temporarily ease my discomfort. Thank you for patiently guiding me to become more healthy and holy every day. In Jesus' name, Amen.

Personal Reflection

Are there any uncomfortable or painful areas of your life in which you would like to see change? Pray and ask God to show you the true source of the discomfort. Ask the Spirit to show you if he is leading you toward an external change, such as location or profession, or if he wants to resolve your discomfort through internal healing and growth. Ask God to show you a few steps you can begin taking this week.

_____

_____

_____

_____

_____

_____

_____

_____

_____

_____

_____

_____

Day 7
Crepe Myrtles

The armyworms and rabbits weren't the only pest in the summer of 2021. My massive crepe myrtles developed a bark scale. Bark scale doesn't sound that bad, but it looks horrific. The scale is caused by tiny insects that secrete a waxy substance, which causes the bark to turn black. In extreme cases, the scale becomes so severe that the bark appears to bleed from white pustules. Even worse, the substance secreted by the insect is sweet, so it attracts more bugs, creating a vicious cycle that destroys the tree.

Like the scale that attracts more bugs, the sin in our lives causes us to spiral into further damaging behavior. You see, sin and disobedience are ultimately self-destructive. In chapter 1, the author of Proverbs warns that sin entices people to sin all the more. He describes what happens to people who get stuck in the downward spiral of sin: "But these people set an ambush for themselves; they are trying to get themselves killed," (Prov 1:18). Allowing sin to take root in our hearts is like setting a trap for ourselves.

Even worse, sin not only devours our own life, but harms the people around us. That ichor-like goo on my crepe myrtles wasn't self-contained. It dripped on all the surrounding plants, turning them black and sticky. In a similar fashion, even when we think our sin is only hurting ourselves, or is a well-kept secret, it always impacts the ones we love. The enemy of our soul seeks to deceive us, lead us out of God's protection, and devour everything good in our lives.

With intense effort, I was able to save the crepe myrtles. I had to apply two different types of pesticide—one to the soil and another to the bark. Then, I had to cut down all the surrounding plants and bushes. Finally, my husband had to help me pressure wash the crepe myrtle. You read that correctly. We pressure washed my garden.

The effort I put into saving the trees is a perfect analogy for the effort required to eradicate ingrained sin. The process will be long, hard, and tedious, and you'll probably need some help to get through it. God will always be there to help you, but he'd rather save you the trouble before it happens.

Lord, thank you for providing guidance in your Word. Thank you for giving me instructions on how to live an abundant life. Help me to turn from any behaviors that do not honor you. Help me to deal with sin before it takes root in my heart. Guide me as I seek to grow in sanctification and holiness. In Jesus' name, Amen.

Personal Reflection

Are you harboring any behaviors that may dishonor God and take root in your heart? Ask God to show you the path that leads to life rather than death. Ask him to reveal any sins of which you may not even be aware. If you have time, read Genesis 3:1–4:16. You may want to take some written or mental notes on the causes and results of sin.

Scan the QR code for passages of Scripture

Day 7

_____

_____

_____

_____

_____

_____

_____

_____

_____

_____

_____

_____

_____

_____

_____

_____

_____

_____

Day 8
Here Comes the Rain Again

Typically, rain is a blessing for gardeners. Not only does rainwater keep the water bill low, but it helps plants grow better than processed water. Water from the tap or hose contains chemicals used to prevent bacterial and fungal contamination. These chemicals like chlorine and fluorine make tap water safe to drink, but they also make it harsh for plants. So, when plants are watered by the clean, fresh rainwater they grow more quickly and thrive.

You may have guessed that during that disastrous summer of 2021, the rainwater was not a blessing for my garden. Our region is usually dry and sunny during the summer, but in 2021, the rain seemed to pour without ceasing. The incessant moisture was, in fact, a major contributor to the bark scale and armyworm outbreak. Adding insult to injury, my vegetables wouldn't produce because they never saw the sun.

Scripture affirms the principle that too much of a good thing can turn into a bad thing. The author of Proverbs warns, "Do you like honey? Don't eat too much, or it will make you sick," (Proverbs 25:16). Our wise sage extolls the benefits of moderation, with which I often struggle. I have trouble doing anything in moderation. My dedication helps me during challenging seasons, like finishing a PhD. But my lack of moderation has also resulted in some negatives. I love to exercise, but nearly all my joints are worn out from exercising too much. I love to garden, but maintaining my copious landscaping costs a great deal of time and money. I rarely can find the middle ground.

God wants to protect us from the consequences of going to extremes. Moreover, he even helps us in our weaknesses. Paul teaches that God's grace covers our mistakes and that his power is perfected in our weakness. Our failings help us lean into the Lord's strength so that his power is evident to the world (2 Corinthians 12:9–10). Furthermore, the Holy Spirit provides self-control and gently corrects us when we go too far (Galatians 5:22–23). Let's take advantage of the faithful support our Father provides.

Jesus, Thank you for providing the gift of the Holy Spirit, who helps me overcome the tendency to overindulge. Please bring to my awareness any behaviors in which I am failing to exercise moderation. I pray that I would seek the comfort and peace of your presence rather than finding temporary fulfillment from external sources. Help me to grow in self-control as I seek to exercise wisdom and draw closer to you. In Jesus' name, Amen.

Personal Reflection

In which areas of your life do you tend to overindulge? Food, work, substances, shopping, sleeping? Ask the Spirit to help you identify one or two behaviors and steps toward moderation.

Day 8
Here Comes the Rain Again

Typically, rain is a blessing for gardeners. Not only does rainwater keep the water bill low, but it helps plants grow better than processed water. Water from the tap or hose contains chemicals used to prevent bacterial and fungal contamination. These chemicals like chlorine and fluorine make tap water safe to drink, but they also make it harsh for plants. So, when plants are watered by the clean, fresh rainwater they grow more quickly and thrive.

You may have guessed that during that disastrous summer of 2021, the rainwater was not a blessing for my garden. Our region is usually dry and sunny during the summer, but in 2021, the rain seemed to pour without ceasing. The incessant moisture was, in fact, a major contributor to the bark scale and armyworm outbreak. Adding insult to injury, my vegetables wouldn't produce because they never saw the sun.

Scripture affirms the principle that too much of a good thing can turn into a bad thing. The author of Proverbs warns, "Do you like honey? Don't eat too much, or it will make you sick," (Proverbs 25:16). Our wise sage extolls the benefits of moderation, with which I often struggle. I have trouble doing anything in moderation. My dedication helps me during challenging seasons, like finishing a PhD. But my lack of moderation has also resulted in some negatives. I love to exercise, but nearly all my joints are worn out from exercising too much. I love to garden, but maintaining my copious landscaping costs a great deal of time and money. I rarely can find the middle ground.

God wants to protect us from the consequences of going to extremes. Moreover, he even helps us in our weaknesses. Paul teaches that God's grace covers our mistakes and that his power is perfected in our weakness. Our failings help us lean into the Lord's strength so that his power is evident to the world (2 Corinthians 12:9–10). Furthermore, the Holy Spirit provides self-control and gently corrects us when we go too far (Galatians 5:22–23). Let's take advantage of the faithful support our Father provides.

Jesus, Thank you for providing the gift of the Holy Spirit, who helps me overcome the tendency to overindulge. Please bring to my awareness any behaviors in which I am failing to exercise moderation. I pray that I would seek the comfort and peace of your presence rather than finding temporary fulfillment from external sources. Help me to grow in self-control as I seek to exercise wisdom and draw closer to you. In Jesus' name, Amen.

Personal Reflection

In which areas of your life do you tend to overindulge? Food, work, substances, shopping, sleeping? Ask the Spirit to help you identify one or two behaviors and steps toward moderation.

_____

_____

_____

_____

Day 9
Soil Samples

Dirt isn't just dirt. Soil is full of various nutrients, so adding fertilizer to your soil can increase the health and productivity of your garden. But have you ever looked at the fertilizer aisle at a gardening store? So many different types of fertilizer are available that I'm always paralyzed by indecision.

This year, I decided to remedy my paralysis. Auburn University has a Soil, Forage, and Water Testing Laboratory to which anyone can send samples. So, I boxed up a scoop of dirt and mailed it away. When I got the results a couple of weeks later, I found out exactly which nutrients were in my soil and in what proportions. The analysis also included a list of fertilizer types that would best supplement my soil. Equipped with new knowledge, I can start my next gardening season primed for maximal results.

You've probably heard the saying "knowledge is power." But according to scripture knowledge and wisdom (applied knowledge) result in protection, good judgment, and honor.

Get wisdom; develop good judgment.
Don't forget my words or turn away from them.
Don't turn your back on wisdom, for she will
protect you.
Love her, and she will guard you.
Getting wisdom is the wisest thing you can do!

And whatever else you do, develop good judgment.
If you prize wisdom, she will make you great. Embrace
her, and she will honor you.

Proverbs 4:5–8

God desires that we grow in knowledge and wisdom. As we grow in knowledge, our spiritual and emotional soil becomes healthier. As we become healthier and better equipped to serve God, our service yields fruit. As I live a fruitful life, make wise decisions for myself, and offer wise counsel to others, I bring honor to my Lord. The overflow of my own growth primes the soil in others for the sowing of the Gospel.

Lord, thank you for providing wisdom generously. Help me continue to grow in wisdom and knowledge. Equip me and prepare me for service in my family, in my workplace, and in my community. Help me exercise good judgment so that I can honor you and bless those around me. Give me a desire to grow in knowledge and wisdom daily as I search your Word. In Jesus' name, Amen.

Personal Reflection

God has blessed us with a multitude of avenues by which we can become better equipped. How might you take steps toward growing in wisdom and knowledge? Is God calling you to become more disciplined in the study of your Bible? Is he drawing you to a mentoring relationship? An educational course? A particular book? Ask God to show you how to take the next step of growth.

_____

_____

Day 9

Day 10
Dirt in the Tub

Yesterday, we talked about the soil in my garden, and today we'll talk about the soil in my bathtub. You may be asking, "Why was there dirt in your bathtub?" Believe me, I was asking the same question. But let me rewind and explain that my bathtub is surrounded by plants. I have plants on shelves, hanging from hooks, and balanced around the rim. In the fall and winter, the situation is even more precarious, because my outside plants have to come inside for the winter.

When I initially began seeing the dirt in my tub, I thought that I had bumped a plant or spilled dirt by overwatering. As I cleaned up dirt morning after morning, I concluded that the dirt wasn't caused by a spill. I suspected that something was moving around in my plants at night. By process of elimination, I flooded each pot with water and pesticide. Sure enough, I found a fat grub and a sizable earthworm in two different pots. Apparently, they'd been having a party every night when I went to bed. Unfortunately for them, their mess earned them a swift trip down the drain. (Side note: Don't wash grubs and worms down your drain unless you want a clog.)

As Christ followers, the evidence we leave in our wake also provides information about our identity. Jesus explains that "A good tree produces good fruit, and a bad tree produces bad fruit. A good tree can't produce bad fruit, and a bad tree can't produce good fruit," (Matthew 7:17–18). In this passage, fruit represents our actions, while the tree represents our identity. If our identity is rooted in the goodness

43

of Christ, our fruit will be healthy and nourishing. Conversely, if our fruit is rotten, our identity likely is rooted in an unhealthy tree.

Internalizing this principle can help us grow in two ways. First, the fruit an individual produces is a reflection of their heart. Although we should never judge or condemn, we might not want to foster an intimate relationship with someone whose fruit is rotten. Similarly, even if someone has a loving heart, if their life is so dysfunctional that they leave a mess of wormy mud in their wake, we should probably stay out of their path.

Second, we should evaluate the fruit of our own lives. What does our fruit say about our identity and character? Our relationship with Christ isn't predicated upon our good deeds, but our actions do reveal how closely we are walking with our Savior. Let's produce the beautiful fruit of salvation and love, and leave that wormy, dirty fruit in the trash.

Lord, thank you for salvation, which empowers and equips me to produce good fruit. I ask you to show me if I am producing unhealthy fruit in any area of my life. Help me honestly self-assess whether my actions reflect an identity rooted in you. I pray that my life will leave evidence of your goodness. Give me the discernment to recognize any individual in my life whose heart might be characterized by unhealthy fruit. Show me how I can distance myself while still offering love and grace. In Jesus' name, Amen.

Personal Reflection

Spend some time in honest self-assessment. What do your works say about the condition of your heart? Based solely on your actions, write a list of words that describe your heart. If your fruit doesn't align with the identity of Christ, take some time to confess his character over yourself. Rather than trying harder to do good works, meditate on his great love for you.

Day 11
The Parable of the Sower

The last couple of days we have been talking about dirt and soil. I would be remiss as a Bible teacher if I didn't spend some time on the most noteworthy dirt parable of all time. Rather than paraphrasing for you, I'd like you to read the words of Jesus for yourself.

[Jesus] told many stories in the form of parables, such as this one: "Listen! A farmer went out to plant some seeds. As he scattered them across his field, some seeds fell on a footpath, and the birds came and ate them. Other seeds fell on shallow soil with underlying rock. The seeds sprouted quickly because the soil was shallow. But the plants soon wilted under the hot sun, and since they didn't have deep roots, they died. Other seeds fell among thorns that grew up and choked out the tender plants. Still other seeds fell on fertile soil, and they produced a crop that was thirty, sixty, and even a hundred times as much as had been planted! Anyone with ears to hear should listen and understand . . . The seed that fell on the footpath represents those who hear the message about the Kingdom and don't understand it. Then the evil one comes and snatches away the seed that was planted in their

hearts. The seed on the rocky soil represents those who hear the message and immediately receive it with joy. But since they don't have deep roots, they don't last long. They fall away as soon as they have problems or are persecuted for believing God's word. The seed that fell among the thorns represents those who hear God's word, but all too quickly the message is crowded out by the worries of this life and the lure of wealth, so no fruit is produced. The seed that fell on good soil represents those who truly hear and understand God's word and produce a harvest of thirty, sixty, or even a hundred times as much as had been planted!"

Matthew 13:3–9; 19–23

The condition of our soil, or our heart, determines how we respond to Jesus and his teaching. Our response to Jesus determines the type and amount of fruit we produce. However, we often focus on the fruit before the soil. We try harder to live righteously and do good deeds, but we find ourselves in the same struggles again and again. Instead, Jesus teaches us to cultivate healthy soil that is saturated in the Gospel. When our fruit is ready to harvest from healthy soil, it will be healthy, abundant, and nourishing to others.

Lord, thank you for teaching me how to have a healthy heart that bears good fruit. Help me cultivate healthy soil by cultivating my relationship with you. Help me become more deeply rooted in your goodness and grace so that my faith produces an abundant harvest. I repent of focusing more on my works than your love. In Jesus' name, Amen.

Personal Reflection

First, read through the list you created yesterday. What do the words that describe your fruit say about the condition of your heart? Which of the four soil types most accurately describes your response to Jesus? Second, release any self-condemnation and rejoice that no matter the condition of your heart, your Savior loves you and wants an intimate relationship with you. Finally, thank him for his love and recommit to cultivating healthy soil by spending meaningful time with him daily.

_____

_____

_____

_____

_____

_____

_____

_____

_____

_____

_____

_____

Day 12
Life Cycle of a Seed

When the soil of our heart is healthy, conditions are favorable for production of good fruit. The Gospel functions a bit like a seed, which under the right conditions will sprout, grow, and reproduce. Jesus described those conditions in the parable from Matthew 13 that we read yesterday.

Today, though, I would like to look a little more closely at the process that seeds undergo as they sprout. First, a seed remains hidden in the soil until it is exposed to warmth and water. It begins to absorb water and nutrients as it prepares to sprout. Next, a radicle, the precursor to a root, begins to grow downward into the soil. Shortly thereafter the first shoot begins growing upward, breaches the ground, and continues to grow if the right conditions persist. Finally, once the plant becomes mature, it produces seeds, which continue the cycle of propagation.

The life cycle of a seed parallels the trajectory of a healthy spiritual life. When we are new to faith in Christ, our relationship with him is undeveloped. Just as a small seed absorbs nutrients, we learn more about the Kingdom of God, the Gospel of Christ, a relationship with Jesus, and our newfound faith. Soon, our roots begin to grow as our faith becomes established. As our roots grow stronger, we can then extend outward shoots, discovering our spiritual gifts and sampling different ways to serve God and others. Like a young plant, we bear healthy fruit, but in small quantities. As we grow into maturity, we discover our purpose, walk in our calling, and bear an abundance of fruit. The fruit of our relationship with Christ yields a bountiful harvest from which seeds of the Gospel are planted in the lives of others.

Just as a mature plant needs healthy soil, water, and nutrients to remain healthy, so also our relationship with Christ requires care. Even mature plants will wither if the soil in which they are rooted becomes unhealthy. Let's diligently tend the soil of our relationship with Jesus by being intentional, studying Scripture, spending time in prayer, and meditating on his Word daily. There is simply no shortcut to fruitful faith.

Lord, thank you for patiently loving me. I repent of neglecting the soil of my heart. Help me to rightly prioritize disciplines that nourish my relationship with you. Help me to keep my spiritual life in good health by fostering inner wholeness prior to outward acts of service. I pray that as I grow in maturity, you will show me where and how to plant the seeds of the Gospel so that others may know you. In Jesus' name, Amen.

Personal Reflection

Continue focusing inward and tending to the soil of your heart. Think of a time in your past during which you felt especially close to God. In just a moment, close your eyes and immerse yourself in that memory. What sounds, sights, smells, tastes or even physical sensations were part of that memory? Savor the physical and emotional impressions without feeling the need to express yourself in words.

_____

_____

_____

_____

Day 13
In the Beginning

Some passages of Scripture are so familiar that we almost ignore them. Take, for example, Genesis 1:1, "In the beginning God created the heavens and the earth." Of course, we know that God is a creator, but we seldom meditate on the creative aspect of God's character. Yet, Scripture repeatedly brings attention to God's creative power. The Psalmist, in particular, offers poetic reflections on the creative activity of God. One striking example is Psalm 104.

> *You placed the world on its foundation*
> *so it would never be moved.*
> *You clothed the earth with floods of water,*
> *water that covered even the mountains.*
> *At your command, the water fled;*
> *at the sound of your thunder, it hurried away.*
> *Mountains rose and valleys sank*
> *to the levels you decreed.*
> *Then you set a firm boundary for the seas,*
> *so they would never again cover the earth.*
> *You make springs pour water into the ravines,*
> *so streams gush down from the mountains.*
> *They provide water for all the animals,*
> *and the wild donkeys quench their thirst.*

> *The birds nest beside the streams*
> *and sing among the branches of the trees.*
>
> ### *Psalm 104:5–12*

The Psalmist was rightly awed at God's beautiful creation as well as his creative power.

Just as God created the natural world, he also created humanity, but unlike the natural world, humans are fashioned in God's image. Being created in God's image doesn't mean that we have a head, two arms, two hands, two legs, and two feet. Being made in the image of God means that we reflect his character and steward his authority. The Psalmist muses upon our role as image bearers.

> *What are mere mortals that you should think about them,*
> *human beings that you should care for them?*
> *Yet you made them only a little lower than God*
> *and crowned them with glory and honor.*
> *You gave them charge of everything you made,*
> *putting all things under their authority.*
>
> ### *Psalm 8:4–6*

As bearers of his image, God has blessed us with the capacity to create life and care for creation. Like God, we can create both tangible objects and abstract entities. God created the earth, but he also created love and friendship. You may create beautiful music and art or create joy by encouraging others. Maybe you are an engineer who enjoys designing machinery, buildings, or other technology. Perhaps you create growth in others through writing, teaching, or serving. Just as important, if not more, we are all called to create strong relationships; we are called to create opportunities for people to hear about the love of Jesus; we are called to create ways to help those who are hurting.

Jesus, in his time on this earth, was also a creator. He was a carpenter by profession, and that certainly isn't a coincidence. He also created a way for us to be free of our sins and to have a relationship with our Heavenly Father. Let's follow his example and walk in our creative faculties today.

Lord, thank you for creating a beautiful world for your children to inhabit. Thank you for allowing me to reflect your creative capacity. Please help me bear your image well. Guide me as I seek to bring you glory through what I create with my life. Empower me as I seek to create opportunities to spread your love and grace. In Jesus' name, Amen.

Personal Reflection

Meditate on your capacity to reflect the creative character of God. What has he gifted you to create? What new expression of creativity can you experiment with today?

_____

_____

_____

_____

_____

_____

_____

_____

_____

Day 14
God Is My Rock

I love visiting Israel in the fall because the heat isn't so brutal. During my last trip, just before the pandemic, I took advantage of the cooler temperatures and worked up the courage to run the "Snake Path" at Masada. The Snake Path is one of the most iconic hikes in Israel, consisting of roughly 700 steps and over 1,000 feet of elevation up the side of a mountain fortress. Standing at the base, I could easily understand why the ancient writers of Scripture compared God to a fortress in passages such as Psalm 62:1–2:

> *I wait quietly before God,*
> *for my victory comes from him.*
> *He alone is my rock and my salvation,*
> *my fortress where I will never be shaken.*

To deepen our understanding of God as a Rock, Salvation, and Fortress, let me tell you a bit about the history of Masada. Toward the end of the New Testament period, the Jewish people rebelled against Rome. Although Rome had continually pressured the Jewish people to worship their emperors and false gods, tensions reached a breaking point around AD 70. Judea rebelled, and Rome moved to enforce the peace, or *Pax Romana*, which was maintained by brutal force. As the Roman military wiped out Jerusalem, surviving Judeans scattered to the countryside. Everywhere they fled, Roman soldiers hunted them down.

One area to which many Jewish families fled was Masada. At the time, the walls of the mountain fortress were so steep that it was completely impervious to invaders. Because the Jewish rebels had plenty of food and water, they were safe from Roman soldiers. Not to be deterred, the Roman military laid siege to Masada for months. With the wealth and power of an empire behind them, the Roman military eventually conquered. Using both soldiers and slave labor, the Romans constructed a siege ramp so massive that it is still visible today, nearly 2000 years later. I'll let you look up the end of the story on your own, but Masada still stands as a monument to Jewish heroism and fortitude.

So, let's return to our original thought: What does it mean that God is our Rock, our Salvation, and our Fortress? First, God gives us protection and rest when we face trials. We can run to him and find the refreshing that our soul needs. Second, God provides for our practical needs. Just as the Jewish people found food, water, and shelter at Masada, God provides for our everyday, practical needs. Third, God is STRONG! Although Rome was eventually able to breach the walls of Masada, they needed legions of soldiers and thousands of slaves working seven days a week to build a ramp to the steep mountain heights.

Our God is even bigger and stronger than Masada, one of the most secure fortresses in all of world history. Unlike Masada, however, God will never be shaken, he will never be defeated, and he will always be the rock to which His people can run. What are you battling today? Turn to God to find the strength and refreshing that your soul needs.

Lord, thank you for being the Rock in whom I can find strength, my Fortress in whom I can find safety, and my Salvation in whom I can find rest. I repent of treating you with less honor than you deserve. Help me to seek refuge in you when I struggle rather than trying to solve problems in my own strength. I confess that my current trials will become a future testimony of your power. I pray that my faith throughout my hardships will encourage others to trust in you. In Jesus' name, Amen.

Personal Reflection

What battles or struggles are you currently facing? Are you trusting God to reveal the right solution in his perfect timing? Have you taken matters into your own hands and tried to find solutions that conflict with the wisdom of Scripture? Are you trusting God to be your protector or are you consumed by worry and doubt? One at a time, entrust each battle into the capable hands of your Father. Confess aloud, if possible, your trust in his provision and protection through each circumstance.

Day 15
Mud Bath

Just down the mountain from Masada, the Dead Sea rests at the lowest point on the globe. Famed as one of the saltiest bodies of water on Earth, its salt concentration is approximately ten times higher than that of sea water. Due to the high salt and mineral content, the Dead Sea has extensive therapeutic benefits.

People from all over the world travel to the Dead Sea to float in the water and coat their bodies in the mineral-rich mud. With more than 30% mineral content, the water is so dense that it feels like oil. In fact, the thickness of the water causes you to float as soon as you walk a few feet from the shore. The natural buoyancy combined with the mineral salts in the water serve to reduce joint inflammation, improve circulation, and reduce muscle stiffness. Additionally, bromide salts in the water act as a natural sedative.

The salty mud beneath the water is likewise curative. The thick, black slime promotes skin health by extracting impurities, improving elasticity, and reducing inflammation. It serves as an effective treatment for acne, psoriasis, and cellulite, among other ailments.

The health benefits of the Dead Sea were well known in Jesus' lifetime, just as they are now. Jesus drew upon this common knowledge and used the properties of salt as an illustration for spiritual health. Matthew records Jesus saying, "You are the salt of the earth. But what good is salt if it has lost its flavor? Can you make it salty again? It will be thrown out and trampled underfoot as worthless," (Matthew 5:13).

Jesus teaches that you are the salt of the Earth. His purpose for your life is that you act as an agent of healing in the world. Regardless of your specific calling, job, or vocation, Jesus has appointed you to rejuvenate lives. Whether you are an engineer, a pastor, a stay-at-home parent, a student, or a retired Christian living your best life, the primary reason for your existence is bringing healing to the world.

The purifying and rejuvenating properties of the Dead Sea are insignificant in comparison to the healing that Jesus offers. The benefits of the Dead Sea are temporary, but the salvation of God is eternal. The Dead Sea is shrinking, but our Lord offers an endless supply of grace and love. Mud from the Dead Sea is black and slimy, but the love of Jesus makes us fresh and clean.

Lord, thank you for bringing healing and health to my heart. Thank you for helping me grow in character and enabling me to impact my community. Help me be "salty" as I strive to be an agent of healing in the world. Open my eyes to needs and opportunities. Empower me to give life, encouragement, and grace to others. In Jesus' name, Amen.

Personal Reflection

Resolve to be "saltier" today. Be intentional about offering encouragement, kind words, and support to those around you. Seek opportunities to share how Jesus has worked in your life and healed your hurts.

_____

_____

_____

Day 15

Day 16
Desiccated Devotion

Yesterday, we talked about the healing properties of salt and Jesus' call for us to be the salt of the world. We are all called to be agents of healing as we follow Christ. However, salt must be used properly if we hope to reap its benefits.

Salt can cause death and destruction just as easily as it can heal. In general, salt heals by drawing water and impurities from cells. In excess, however, salt causes dehydration, illness, and even death. For snails, slugs, bacteria, and microbes, salt is deadly. If you sprinkle salt over your plants or mix it into your garden soil, the salt will dehydrate plant cells, causing them to wither and die. The salty soil will also prevent future growth from sprouting.

The more concentrated the salt, the greater the potential for healing or harm. The Dead Sea has such a high salt concentration that no life can survive in it, hence the name "Dead Sea." Although the water is healthy for the skin, a few sips can cause vomiting, but only if you don't suffocate and die first.

How does a substance that promotes healing also cause such destruction? The key to reaping the benefits of salt is proper use. Salt must be used in the right manner and in the right context to be effective.

Much like salt, religion can foster healing or harm. Jesus chastised the Pharisees for their toxic legalism.

> *What sorrow awaits you teachers of religious law and*
> *you Pharisees. Hypocrites! For you are careful to tithe*

even the tiniest income from your herb gardens, but you ignore the more important aspects of the law— justice, mercy, and faith. You should tithe, yes, but do not neglect the more important things . . . For you are so careful to clean the outside of the cup and the dish, but inside you are filthy—full of greed and self-indulgence! You blind Pharisee! First wash the inside of the cup and the dish, and then the outside will become clean, too . . . For you are like whitewashed tombs— beautiful on the outside but filled on the inside with dead people's bones and all sorts of impurity.

Matthew 23:23, 25–27

The religious legalism of the Pharisees sucked the joy out of their relationship with God. Even worse, they dispersed deadly salt by modeling desiccated faith. Instead of spreading healing and life, they fostered dysfunction in those to whom they ministered. Anyone can soak up Scripture like the Pharisees, yet still be dead inside. Legalism never leads to life.

James, the brother of Jesus, shows us how to spread salt in a way that brings life instead of death. He instructs us to obey God in our words and deeds, model a life of integrity, live in purity, and extend kindness. He calls us to love and serve people who can't help themselves, who are weak, and who are poor. James exhorts us to confess our sins, pray for one another, and persevere through trials (James 1–5). Unlike the dead religion of the Pharisees, a healthy relationship with Christ seasons the life of everyone around us.

Lord, thank you for teaching me how to have a healthy, life-giving relationship with you. Help me obey you in a spirit of love rather than legalism. Guide me as I seek to live a holy life so that I can bring healing to those around me. Grow my desire to serve others and help those who are weak. Help me grow in humility so that I bring greater glory to you than myself. Remind me to be salty in a positive way every day so that I can season my world with love and grace. In Jesus' name, Amen.

Personal Reflection

Continue aspiring to be "salty" today. Seek opportunities to extend kindness, serve others, and meet needs in tangible ways.

_____

_____

_____

_____

_____

_____

_____

_____

_____

_____

_____

_____

Day 17
Salty Speech

The last couple of days we've talked about the properties of salt. As followers of Christ, we are called to spread the curative benefits of salt to our world. In Colossians, Paul teaches specifically that we should season our words with salt (Colossians 4:6). How can we do that more effectively?

Think about salt as a seasoning. I've never met anyone who doesn't like their food seasoned with salt. I use lots of salt, I mean, a lot. I rarely use condiments or salad dressing because salt provides all the flavor I need. Instead of dipping fries in ketchup, I dip them in salt. I can get away with it because I need the electrolytes for my strenuous exercise routine. Of course, salt can be unhealthy if used improperly, but we talked about that yesterday.

When used properly, salt offers amazing benefits. In addition to the healing properties we have already discussed, salt is essential for bodily functions. A salt deficiency can cause low blood pressure, seizures, heart attacks, dehydration, and even death. Salt promotes a healthy nervous system by facilitating electrical conduction in the body's nerves. For those of us who are fitness junkies, salt helps balance electrolytes and prevents muscle cramping.

So, how can we season our words with salt? Let me offer a few suggestions. First, season your words with moderation. Don't talk too much or too little. If you never talk about your faith, you are depriving people of Jesus. Yet, if you talk too much, you'll annoy people, and they'll start to tune you out. Second, season your words with grace. The kindness of God attracts people to him, not hellfire and damnation (Romans 2:4). Extend the grace and kindness of God liberally. Third, season your words with joy. Just as we salt our food to make it tastier, we can season our conversations in such a way that they are enjoyable. When we offer the encouragement, truth, love, and acceptance of God, people want to experience more of him. Fourth, season your words with life. Our words can lead people to an abundant life of freedom in Christ, or our words can cause destruction and death (Proverbs 18:21). Rather than pointing out problems, let's draw attention to the opportunities God has placed before us. Rather than pointing out flaws, let's draw attention to the beautiful qualities with which God has endowed each individual.

The words we speak are not neutral, and every conversation has an impact. Let's follow the recipe that Scripture provides so that each interaction is exquisitely seasoned with life, love, and joy.

Lord, thank you for allowing me to be a healing and purifying influence on the world. Help me be more discerning and intentional about the impact of my words. Give me the self-control to stop any hurtful words before they can proceed from my mouth. Fill my heart with life and love so that my words are an overflow of the joy in my heart. Open my eyes to opportunities to encourage those who are hurting. Give me the courage to share my faith with those who don't know you. In Jesus' name, Amen.

Personal Reflection

Continue aspiring to be "salty" today. Be intentional about seeking opportunities to offer encouragement, kind words, and support to those around you.

Day 17

Day 18
Grab the Reins

Yesterday, we talked about seasoning our words with salt by imbuing our conversations with the love and grace of God. Speech is a crucial concept throughout Scripture, and if the authors of Scripture consider it important, we should pay attention. James, in particular, has much to say about the way we speak. Therefore, we'll spend several days with James learning how to communicate in healthier and holier ways.

James spends almost the entirety of chapter 3 dealing with speech. Like a good teacher, he uses practical examples to drive home his message. Today, we'll focus on the first of James' illustrations. According to James 3:3, "We can make a large horse go wherever we want by means of a small bit in its mouth."

Have you ever seen a bit? The bit is a small piece of metal that goes into a horse's mouth and fits into the space behind the teeth. The small apparatus is connected to the bridle and reins, all three of which function in tandem to create subtle pressure on the horse's mouth cartilage. Because the cartilage is tender and the bit is somewhat uncomfortable, the horse will go exactly where you lead. James is teaching that although the bit is one small component, it can control the whole horse. Let me illustrate the concept with a personal example.

I've always loved riding horses. I'm not an expert horsewoman, I just enjoy the opportunity to ride whenever it arises. While I was growing up, my uncle and aunt in Kentucky had a horse named Bo.

Bo was gentle and well-mannered. His docile nature was fortunate for me, as I was a novice rider.

One summer, when I was around fifteen years old, I went for a ride in the beautiful Kentucky hills. Not long into the ride, Bo decided he was ready to go home and raced into a sprint—at least it felt like a sprint to me. In reality, it was probably a reasonably paced gallop. As a novice rider, however, I panicked and simply hung on for dear life. As we galloped into the yard, my cousin looked at me as if I had gone insane and said, "Use the reins!" In my panic, I had forgotten to control Bo by tightening the reins.

James is teaching us that our tongue is like the bit and reigns of a horse. We can choose to take control, or by default, we will be controlled. We must actively grab the reins, or our tongue will run out of control and take us where we don't want to go.

Although my horseback riding skills are comical, taming the tongue is no laughing matter. Like learning to ride a horse, controlling the tongue requires practice. You won't become an expert overnight, but God will teach you to take firm grip on the reins.

Lord, thank you for continuously teaching me how to speak in a manner that gives life to others and brings glory to you. Help me be more thoughtful and careful as I learn healthier patterns of communication. Teach me to control my speech rather than letting it control me. Teach me to speak words that encourage people and draw them to you. In Jesus' name, Amen.

Personal Reflection

Throughout your day, practice taking the reins and growing in self-control by refraining from any harmful words. As you guard your tongue against hurtful speech, also seek opportunities to offer encouragement, kind words, and support.

Day 19
Taming the Tongue

Yesterday, we talked about the tongue as a small body part that can direct the whole person. James teaches us that like grabbing the reins of a horse, we must actively take control of our speech. Left uncontrolled, the tongue will run wild and take us where we don't want to go. Even worse, James warns that the tongue is nearly impossible to tame. He explains, "People can tame all kinds of animals, birds, reptiles, and fish, but no one can tame the tongue," (James 3:7–8a).

Nearly any animal can be tamed and trained. Domesticated animals like dogs can be trained to track illegal drugs, detect cancer, herd livestock, and serve as guides for the blind. Closer to home, my Gram trained her poodle to fetch the newspaper each morning, and my Dad, an avid duck hunter, trained his Labrador to retrieve. Even wild animals can be trained, although their behavior is more unpredictable. We've probably all heard horror stories about exotic pets turning on their owners and trainers.

James warns that our tongue is harder to tame than the most feral creature on Earth. He cautions, "no one can tame the tongue," and describes our words as an unpredictable force. He warns, "[The tongue] is restless and evil, full of deadly poison. Sometimes it praises our Lord and Father, and sometimes it curses those who have been made in the image of God," (James 3:8b–9).

If you read closely, you'll notice that James is subtly referencing the creation account. In James 3:7, James lists animals that God placed under the stewardship of humans in Genesis 1–2. Then in 3:9, he reminds us that we are created in God's very image. As James evokes the setting of creation, he reminds us that words have power. Our Father used words to create the universe. As his image-bearers, we are also called to use our words in ways that give life.

Conversely, we have the option to use speech destructively. Just as James references Genesis 1–2, he also alludes to the manipulative words of the serpent in Genesis 3. The serpent used his words to deceive Adam and Eve, resulting in a curse on all creation. With his Old Testament callback, James is reminding us that words have a monumental impact, both for good and for evil.

According to James, you have a choice. Will you use words to give life or allow them to create death and destruction? The tongue may be harder to train than a wild animal, but you bear the very image of God. Choose to reflect his image well and imbue your words with his creative power.

Lord, thank you for allowing me to bear your image and speak words that have power to change the world. Help me to reflect your image as I seek to create life and love in my world. Forgive me for speaking words that have distorted your image and caused destruction. In the future, help me refrain from speaking words out of insecurity, anger, pride, or resentment. Fill me with the power of your Spirit so that I can remain self-controlled in moments when I am tempted to speak hurtful words. I pray that each time I speak I would be a blessing to you and to others. In Jesus' name, Amen.

Personal Reflection

Continue refraining from harmful words and offering encouragement throughout your day. Any time you see an animal, tame or wild, let it be a reminder that you bear the image of God and that you have the power to control your tongue.

Day 19

Day 20
Glory in the Storm

Here in the southeast region of the United States, we understand the power of storms. Most of us have lived through tornadoes, if not hurricanes. In Psalm 29, our Psalmist reminds us that God is the Master of nature.

> *Honor the Lord for the glory of his name.*
> *Worship the Lord in the splendor of his holiness.*
> *The voice of the Lord echoes above the sea.*
> *The God of glory thunders.*
> *The Lord thunders over the mighty sea.*
> *The voice of the Lord is powerful;*
> *the voice of the Lord is majestic.*
>
> ### *Psalm 29:2–4*

The psalmist informs us that God rules the storm and that his voice is more powerful than the most turbulent sea. Through the power of nature, the power of God is revealed. Nothing in heaven or on the earth can thwart God's purpose because he is sovereign over all. Our Heavenly Father is easily able to give us victory over anything that might threaten our security. In the light of God's glory, power, and holiness, the Psalmist instructs us to honor and worship the Lord appropriately.

It's easy to skim past the "glory of his name" and miss the importance of God's glory, which is especially relevant in the context of storms. Glory is translated from the Hebrew word *kabod*. *Kabod* literally means heaviness, but in the positive sense of abundance. God is so substantial that no storm can drown out his voice, disrupt his plans, or blow him over.

To illustrate this concept, imagine two piles of rocks. In one pile, we have many pebbles; we have tornadoes, hurricanes, thunderstorms, and floods. In the other pile, we have one large rock that represents the glory of God. No matter how many pebbles you add to the first pile, it simply isn't weighty enough to overcome the glory and power of God.

Let's look at another verse that expresses a similar concept but relates more directly to our lives. In 2 Corinthians 4:17–18, Paul says, "For our present troubles are small and won't last very long. Yet they produce for us a glory that vastly outweighs them and will last forever! So, we don't look at the troubles we can see now; rather, we fix our gaze on things that cannot be seen. For the things we see now will soon be gone, but the things we cannot see will last forever." Paul acknowledges that our present troubles are indeed weighty. He also wants us to understand that our trials produce in us a glory that is eternal and far outweighs our current struggles.

Once again, consider our illustration with the rocks. In the pile of pebbles, we have all the trials of life. We have worries, relationship problems, financial strains, and busy schedules. In the other pile is the large rock that represents the glory of God. Because we are in Christ, the big rock also represents the glory that is available to us. In fact, as we keep our eyes fixed upon the big rock, we become more anchored by God's glory. When we walk through trials and keep our eyes upon God, we become better able to overcome whatever our temporary situation looks like because we have access to God, who supplies an infinite amount of glory.

Lord, I acknowledge that you are worthy of all honor and glory. Help me to grasp the immense weight of your glory and learn to trust you more. I pray that my life would reflect your glory as I navigate the storms of life. Help me to keep my eyes fixed on you throughout my trials so that I can become anchored by your power. Empower me to reflect your glory so that I can be a rock for those around me who are hurting. In Jesus' name, Amen.

Personal Reflection

Recall a trial or struggle you experienced in the past. How did God help you stand firm and navigate your difficult season? How did you grow more like Jesus as a result of your trial? As you encounter the storms of life in the present or in the future, remind yourself of how God helped you overcome past tempests.

_____

_____

_____

_____

_____

_____

_____

_____

_____

Day 21
Glory in Creation

Yesterday we contemplated the glory of God—the weight of his presence. God's anchoring presence helps us withstand the storms of life, but God's glory is more than an inoculation against trials. God's glory is a beautiful, bountiful aspect of his presence. We need only observe the world around us to see the riches of God.

> *The heavens proclaim the glory of God.*
> *The skies display his craftsmanship.*
> *Day after day they continue to speak;*
> *night after night they make him known.*
> *They speak without a sound or word;*
> *their voice is never heard.*
> *Yet their message has gone throughout the earth,*
> *and their words to all the world.*
>
> ### *Psalm 19:1–4*

God fashioned the natural world in such a way that we can experience his glory without needing teachers, books, podcasts, or even sermons. Certainly, the resources we have at our disposal help us learn more about God, but he also makes it possible for us to draw nearer to him simply by observing creation. The sun, moon, and stars testify to the infinitude of his existence. The faithfulness of God is demonstrated by the rising and setting of the sun each day. The creativity and artistry of God are reflected in the vast diversity of animal, insect, and plant life.

Even inanimate aspects of creation like beaches, mountains, and deserts "speak without sound or word" as they testify to his handiwork.

Traditional methods of learning, such as reading and studying, can become dry and tedious at times. However, meditating on God's creation as we experience the natural world keeps our relationship with our Father fresh and stimulating. The voice of God's creation complements the words of Scripture and deepens our love for our Father.

We don't have to wait for a routinely scheduled prayer time, Bible study, or church service to experience God's presence. God is so gracious that he literally surrounds us with his glory. Let's open our eyes, ears, and hearts and experience God's glory afresh through the beauty of his creation.

Lord, thank you for placing a wealth of resources at my disposal. Help me to take advantage of every opportunity to learn more about you and draw closer to you. Help me be more aware of your glory throughout the natural world. Show me how to listen more attentively and learn from your creation. As I savor the beauty of the natural world, please enable me to see you more clearly. In Jesus' name, Amen.

Personal Reflection

Begin to cultivate a habit of observing and meditating upon the natural world. Over the next few days, as you move through your daily routine, observe the world around you. Use the space below to write down a few observations. Do you see anything beautiful, awe-inspiring, strange, funny, confusing, or even frightening? The sky is literally the limit!

_____

_____

Day 21

Day 22

Glory Speaks

To cultivate your practice of experiencing God through the natural world, we'll spend a couple more days discussing how we can best experience God through creation. Scripture is abundantly clear that God communicates with his people through nature. According to Job 12:

> *"But ask the animals, and they will teach you,*
> *or the birds in the sky, and they will tell you;*
> *or speak to the earth, and it will teach you,*
> *or let the fish in the sea inform you.*
> *Which of all these does not know*
> *that the hand of the Lord has done this?*
> *In his hand is the life of every creature*
> *and the breath of all mankind."*
> ### *Job 12:7–10*

Obviously, these verses aren't intended to be taken literally. Even if you chase down a bird and ask it questions about God, you aren't going to learn much, except that birds are hard to catch. So, let's clarify the manner in which we should (and should not) learn from the world around us.

We read books, watch videos, listen to podcasts, and ingest various forms of media on a routine basis. When we do so, we form certain conclusions without conscious thought. If, for example, I see a nature documentary on television, I will conclude that the information delivered is factual. I'll know that I can learn truths about the world and confidently pass those truths on to others. If, however, I watch *Alien Worlds*, I know that the information I ingest is decidedly not factual. Although the Netflix show looks similar to a documentary, it is purely science-fiction. If my goal is to learn about plant and animal life on earth, I will find something different to watch.

My point is that we must learn from nature with the correct set of objectives and conclusions. If you want to learn about God's salvific work throughout history or how God expects his followers to live, you should study Scripture or talk to your pastor. If you "ask the animals" or "speak to the earth" for specific guidance, you will never receive a response (unless you have a profoundly supernatural occurrence). Nature will never speak to you with audible words, facts, proverbs.

We must conclude that God wants us to approach creation with a different objective. Indeed, the verses from Job make our objective clear when we read closely. Job teaches that every creature in the sky, on the land, and in the water, testifies to God's creative work. Our Father fashioned the habitat of each creature, and he holds each life in his hand. When we allow the natural world to speak on its own terms, we learn about our Father and our relationship with him. Because God is powerful enough to create and sustain the entire universe, he is certainly powerful enough to care for you and I and provide for our needs.

We all need to learn facts and truths about the Kingdom of God, yet we also need to bask in the beauty of God's creation and experience his presence. Let's be sure to make time for both.

Lord, thank you for creating a beautiful and hospitable world through which I can learn more about you. Help me to find the right balance between studying your Word and observing your works. Help me to find the right balance between serving you and sitting in your presence. As I gaze upon your creation, cause me to grow in faith and maturity. May my love for you and delight in your works draw others to your presence. In Jesus' name, Amen.

Personal Reflection

Continue cultivating a habit of observing and meditating upon the natural world. Yesterday, you began writing down your thoughts and impressions. Continue taking notes on whatever attracts your attention or creates an emotional response. Begin to pray and ask God what you can learn about him through your observations. There are no "right" or "wrong" answers. Just remember, the message of the natural world will never contradict the message of Scripture.

_____

_____

_____

_____

_____

_____

_____

_____

Day 23
Glory Shines

Over the last few days, we've discussed experiencing the glory and presence of God through creation. As we meditate on his works, we perceive more of his character. Nature testifies to the vast scope of God's power and, at the same time, to his intimate involvement in every aspect of creation. Nonetheless, the created world can't offer specific answers about how to live as a child of God.

While the created world can't speak to the specifics of life and faith, nature does help us experience the presence of the Father and grow in spiritual maturity. Focusing our attention on God removes the focus from our turbulent emotions, racing thoughts, and busy lives (Isaiah 26:3–4). As we continue to gaze upon him, our perspective begins to shift, and our mind begins to clear. For example, the pond behind my house will never tell me whether or not to accept a new job opportunity. However, as I sit by the restful waters, my mind and spirit may become quiet and calm enough to discern God's wisdom. My garden will never be able to offer relationship advice. Yet, if I take some time to work in the soil, my concerns might recede enough for the Holy Spirit to bring a helpful passage of Scripture to mind.

In 2 Corinthians 3, Paul talks about the veil that Moses wore when his face shone with the glory of God. The veil separated the people of Israel from the presence of God, but because of Christ, we no longer need a veil to separate us from God's glory. Paul explains, "So all of us who have had that veil removed can see and reflect the glory of the Lord. And the Lord—who is the Spirit—makes us more and more like him as we are changed into his glorious image," (2 Corinthians 3:18).

Our veil is removed when we accept the salvation of Christ. Yet, through the daily stresses of life, we often slip that veil back on. Spending time with God in nature helps us to shed the veil of worldly thoughts, worries, and behaviors. As we see God's glory through the created world, we can more clearly see ourselves in the light of God's glory. That shining light helps us see God's direction for our lives, and as we walk in his will, we reflect his glory all the more.

Lord, thank you for making yourself known through your creation and your son Jesus. Help me fix my eyes on your glory so that I more clearly reflect your presence to the world each day. Make me aware of anything that is clouding my spiritual eyes and preventing me from seeing you clearly. Give me the strength and discipline to remove anything that is clouding my vision. In Jesus' name, Amen.

Personal Reflection

Continue cultivating a habit of observing and meditating upon the natural world. Continue taking notes on whatever attracts your attention or creates an emotional response. As you pray, ask God what you can learn about him through your observations. Next, ask God what he would have you learn about yourself.

_____

_____

_____

_____

Day 23

Day 24
Banished

When I was a little girl, my sister and I had a favorite movie called "Panda's Great Adventure." The movie was about a young panda facing a rite of passage. Panda was required to overcome various trials of strength and stamina to prove his worth. I don't recall all the details, but I remember that Panda had to climb a high waterfall to complete the final challenge and earn a place among his people. But Panda failed. Unworthy of remaining among his people, Panda was banished from his family and his home.

Panda's exile was heartbreaking. I remember seeing tears streaming down the face of my younger sister. Panda's story made such an emotional impact that we still remember him nearly 40 years later!

Even as very small children, we understand that being cut off from our family and our home is a traumatic fate. What is worse, each of us begins life banished from God. Thankfully, our Heavenly Father takes the initiative to reestablish a relationship. Second Samuel 14 says, "[God] devises ways to bring us back when we have been separated from him," (2 Samuel 14:14b).

God doesn't require us to prove ourselves by feats of strength, skill, and intellect. Through the work of Jesus on the cross, we are all made worthy when we accept his love and grace. Through Christ, God has devised a way for each of his banished children to return home.

Maybe you feel out of sorts or are searching for purpose. Maybe you feel lonely or afraid. Maybe you feel frustrated or angry. Return to the loving arms of your Father. In Psalm 91, the Psalmist says that God will shelter you, protect you, and calm your fears.

Before we close today, I want to assure you that everything worked out for Panda. He trained hard, returned home, and climbed that waterfall. He was deemed worthy and accepted back into the fold. I'm so glad that God loves me even when I am weak and unworthy. I am so thankful that I don't have to earn the forgiveness of Christ, and that he accepts me just as I am.

Lord, thank you for your unconditional grace in my life. Thank you for sheltering me when I am weak and protecting me from harm. Please help me remember that I don't have to earn my way into your love, and that you love me just as I am. Give me opportunities to share the good news of your Love. In Jesus' name, Amen.

Personal Reflection

Finding the right balance between grace and effort in our walk with Christ requires attention and care. During different seasons of our lives, we may lean toward one extreme or the other. Consider your own walk with Jesus. Do you strive to please God through obedience, service, and works or do you use your freedom in Christ as a license to do whatever you want? How can you find a healthier balance between the two extremes?

_____

_____

_____

_____

Day 25
Open the Floodgates

A couple of years ago, our water heater sprung a leak. To make matters worse, the water heater is in our attic, above one of the bedrooms. On the day of the leak, we turned the water off and quickly called a plumber to the house. He examined the area and concluded that the leak was contained in the pan beneath the water heater. So, with great relief, we planned to have a new water heater installed the next morning and went about our business.

Later that evening, our son, Asher, came into our bedroom to let us know that his ceiling was dripping. Clearly the leak had not been contained within the pan. We couldn't do anything about the drip at 10:30pm, so we placed buckets under the leaks and instructed Asher to sleep in another room.

The next morning, a crew arrived to install the new water heater. As Wesley and I were making phone calls and trying to formulate a plan for repairing water damage, we heard a loud crash from Asher's room. We both ran to the bedroom to find that the entire ceiling had collapsed. Water, wet insulation, and ceiling chunks covered everything. It was a nightmare!

The water heater debacle is an excellent illustration of Proverbs 17:14. The sage teaches, "Starting a quarrel is like opening a floodgate, so stop before a dispute breaks out," (Proverbs 17:14). A quarrel begins like a small leak. Perhaps we have differing opinions or get annoyed with one another. If we don't quickly stop the drip by finding a peaceful solution, the leak will get bigger and bigger. Then, as the leak widens, we get seriously angry. We might yell at one another or refuse to speak. As the conflict escalates, we progress to personal attacks and hurtful words. At that point, the water is pouring through the rift, and we are so furious that we have no desire to make amends. Finally, we do or say something that causes deep hurt and lasting damage, and everything comes crashing down.

Fortunately, the author of Proverbs provides a simple strategy for avoiding conflict. He teaches us that "A gentle answer deflects anger, but harsh words make tempers flare," (Proverbs 15:1). Before tempers flare and water starts leaking, kind words have the potential to throttle anger and plug any drips. Rather than escalating a conflict with angry words, we have the capacity to defuse the situation with gentleness.

I know it isn't always easy to speak kind words in the midst of conflict. Kind words are difficult to offer toward those who hurt us. But with practice, discipline, and the help of the Holy Spirit, we can bring peace to nearly any difficult situation.

Lord, thank you for allowing me to reflect your character by being a peacemaker. Help me be aware of how my own words impact those around me, especially in moments of tension. I repent of speaking words with the intent to harm or manipulate. Help me resist the desire to win arguments at the expense of relationships. Teach me to speak words that defuse tense situations, soothe anger, and bring reconciliation. In Jesus' name, Amen.

Personal Reflection

Becoming more aware of your own speech patterns in moments of conflict is the first step toward cultivating healthier patterns of communication. How do you typically respond when you feel angry, attacked, underappreciated, or ignored? Throughout your day today, practice being more intentional and thoughtful about the words you speak in moments of tension.

_____

_____

_____

_____

_____

_____

_____

_____

_____

_____

_____

_____

_____

_____

_____

Day 26
Crunchy Snacks

Today I am going to share a deep dark secret with you. Until recently, very few people outside of my family knew of this shameful habit from my childhood. Are you ready?

When I was a toddler, I loved to eat bugs. I remember crawling from windowsill to windowsill looking for bugs to eat. I also remember that the old, dry, dead bugs were the best because they were crunchy. My mom will tell you that she remembers catching me with cricket legs hanging out of my mouth. Although my instinct was to gobble up those crunchy little morsels, she lovingly and gently taught me a better way. I still love crunchy snacks, but I learned that there were much tastier foods to eat than bugs.

Our loving Heavenly Father also teaches us, his children, to learn and grow. John exhorts, "See how much the Father has loved us! His love is so great that we are called God's children—and so, in fact, we are. This is why the world does not know us: it has not known God. My dear friends, we are now God's children, but it is not yet clear what we shall become. But we know that when Christ appears, we shall be like him, because we shall see him as he really is," (1 John 3:1–2).

As we mature, we become more like Christ, and our transformation will be complete when he returns. In the meantime, however, John provides insight into our transformation process. In 1 John 3:9, he writes, "Those who have been born into God's family do not make a practice of sinning, because God's life is in them. So they can't keep on sinning, because they are children of God," (1 John 3:9). This verse is sometimes misunderstood to mean that after we accept Christ, we never again sin. Yet, the larger context of scripture is clear that we must continually be wary of slipping into sin. John is actually teaching that through God's fatherly love and guidance, we learn to walk in healthy patterns of life. In other words, I won't keep crawling on the ground eating bugs. My loving heavenly Father gently lifts me up and shows me a better way. Furthermore, as a good parent, God teaches me a little at a time. He doesn't expect me to be perfect overnight, but he does call me to continually grow and mature. So, let's seek God together and ask him how he would have us grow today.

Lord, thank you for loving me as a Father and gently helping me grow in maturity. I repent of holding onto bad habits because they are familiar. I pray that any behaviors that do not honor you would be as abhorrent to me as eating bugs. Help me to receive the guidance of your Holy Spirit with humility and grace. I pray that my growth will never become stagnant, but that I will become like Christ daily. In Jesus' name, Amen.

Personal Reflection

Sometimes we maintain patterns of behavior that, while not technically sinful, are not beneficial. Foster the habit of seeking God's guidance at a deeper level and ask him to show you any patterns of behavior that are impeding your growth. Then, ask him how you can replace those behaviors with habits that will take you to greater levels of maturity.

_____

_____

Day 27
Sweet Home Alabama

"Home" is a word that evokes feelings of warmth for many people. My home state, Alabama, provides feelings of warmth quite literally almost year-round. Although I love to travel quite frequently, coming back to "sweet home Alabama" always brings me joy. The warm weather, red clay, vast cotton fields, and dense forests are in my blood. What brings me the most joy isn't the place but the people. My family is what makes Alabama my home, especially my husband, Wesley, and my two teenage boys, Asher and Abel.

In Scripture, we learn that "this world is not our permanent home" (Hebrews 13:14). We eagerly anticipate eternal paradise in a heavenly setting. We often imagine heaven as a paradise where we float on clouds, take naps, and play harps. However, heaven isn't about *where* we are going, but *who* will be there. In John 14, Jesus says, "There is more than enough room in my Father's home. If this were not so, would I have told you that I am going to prepare a place for you? When everything is ready, I will come and get you, so that you will always be with me where I am," (John 14:2–3).

The authors of Scripture offer shockingly little information about what heaven will be like, but they repeatedly stress that we will be with our Father God and our Lord Jesus. Even though we aren't experiencing heaven yet, we have a foretaste through God's Spirit. We can take part in the joy, comfort, and peace of our eternal home right here and now. Indeed, Jesus promises the gift of the Spirit in John 14.

Jesus replied, "All who love me will do what I say.
My Father will love them, and we will come and
make our home with each of them . . . But when
the Father sends the Advocate as my representa-
tive—that is, the Holy Spirit—he will teach you
everything and will remind you of everything I have
told you. I am leaving you with a gift—peace of mind
and heart. And the peace I give is a gift the world
cannot give. So don't be troubled or afraid."

John 14:23, 26–27

The Holy Spirit enables us to abide in the presence of God at all times. Even though we aren't with our Lord bodily, we can remain at home in his presence.

Think about a family vacation. We may leave Alabama, but we still enjoy the feeling of home because we are together. No matter where we are geographically, we take joy and peace in each other's presence. Likewise, when we abide in the presence of our Father, we can dwell in his joy, peace, and love no matter where we are.

Lord, thank you for sending your Holy Spirit to lead me and teach me. Forgive me for becoming complacent and comfortable in my earthly home while neglecting to seek the shelter of my heavenly home in your presence. Help me to abide in your joy, dwell in your peace, and share your love. Make me aware of opportunities to invite others into your heavenly presence. In Jesus' Name, Amen.

Personal Reflection

Practice abiding in God's presence today. Set an hourly reminder on your watch, calendar, or mobile device to seek his guidance, rest in his peace, give thanks for your blessings, or ask him to fill your heart with his joy.

_____

_____

_____

_____

_____

_____

_____

_____

_____

_____

_____

_____

_____

Day 28
Fields of Cotton

In Alabama, fields of cotton abound in the fall. In some areas, cotton blooms spread as far as the eye can see. So, on one lovely day in September, I decided to pick a few for my nature-loving son, Abel. As expected, he was delighted to receive the cotton, and planned to make a small hand towel from the fibers. First, however, Abel had to remove numerous seeds from the white, fluffy balls. Once his task was complete, he began watching tutorials on how to make fabric from scratch. Unfortunately, Abel discovered that he had removed the seeds incorrectly and ruined the cotton. He was quite disappointed and asked me to procure more cotton for him. By this time, however, the cotton had been harvested and only tiny wisps of white could be found on the plants.

Desiring to encourage Abel's creative endeavor, I went on a mission to find more cotton. I drove down country road after country road until I found one small patch that had not been harvested. If you've ever seen a cotton plant up close and personal, you know that they are quite thorny. So, in the process of procuring cotton for Abel, my legs got scratched up and my fingers were pricked over and over again. I'm sure I went home with some fresh bug bites as well. Yet, I didn't mind because I love my son, and I wanted to make him happy.

The inconveniences I faced are trivial in the light of the sacrifices God made on behalf of his children. The prophet Isaiah tells us that Jesus "was pierced for our rebellion, crushed for our sins. He was beaten so we could be whole. He was whipped so we could be healed,"

(Isaiah 53:5). Jesus was literally pierced, beaten, and killed. He went to great lengths to demonstrate his love and save us from an eternity without him. He gave himself freely and without reservation.

Although such great love is hard to imagine, the love of Christ is far greater than the love I have for my children. Abel never did create that hand towel, but I wasn't upset with him. The purpose of my sacrifice wasn't to get something in return. Likewise, Jesus doesn't need you to earn his love. You already have it. So today, rather than defining your relationship with Jesus by what you can or cannot do, take time to bask in his love. Thank him and tell him you love him too. When our faith is rooted in love, nothing can separate us from our Savior (Romans 8:35–39).

Lord, thank you for sacrificing yourself out of your great love for me. Thank you for enduring unimaginable suffering on my behalf. I ask that you help me to live out my faith in the light of your love, rather than fear or obligation. Grow my love for you as I walk the path you've placed before me. In Jesus' Name, Amen.

Personal Reflection

Think about the people you love the most. Meditate on the truth that Jesus' love for you is deeper than your greatest love. Read Isaiah 53:5 again, but put your name in the place of the personal pronouns. As you thank him for the sacrifice he made on your behalf, ask him to refresh your love for him.

_____

_____

_____

Day 29

Meet My Dogs

Few things in life bring me more joy than my dogs, so I think it's about time I introduced them to you. Smokey and Pepper, brother and sister, are mini schnauzers. We jovially call them "jumbo minis" because they are huge for mini schnauzers at about 35 pounds each. Smokey is tall, regal, dashing, and loves people. Pepper is short, portly, and ratty looking by comparison. When guests visit our home, she growls at them and then retreats to her hideout under our bed.

In the more conspicuous ways, Smokey seems to be a much better dog. He is more handsome, friendly, and even tempered. Yet, Smokey has caused his share of problems. My dapper boy is massively injury prone and has required several major surgeries. His broken leg at four months old cost us literally thousands of dollars.

Because of Smokey's leg injury, he has never enjoyed long walks or jogs. Thus, Pepper is my best friend on the trails. Her rotund little body can hang tough for hours. Plus, since she doesn't like strangers, I know she will keep me safe from any creepers.

Despite their individual flaws, I adore each of my pups. I delight in their funny personalities and overlook frustrations that they cause. They are part of my family, and our home would be incomplete without them.

You are part of God's family, and he loves you even more than I love my dogs! God created you uniquely and loves you unconditionally. He knows that you have flaws, and he adores you anyway.

But God is so rich in mercy, and he loved us so much, that even though we were dead because of our sins, he gave us life when he raised Christ from the dead. (It is only by God's grace that you have been saved!) . . . For we are God's masterpiece. He has created us anew in Christ Jesus, so we can do the good things he planned for us long ago.

Ephesians 2:4–5, 10

God created us with beautiful differences. We each have our own strengths and weaknesses, likes and dislikes. God has given you a specific purpose for which you are ideally created, and which no one else can adequately fulfill.

You will find great fulfillment as you embrace your unique design, but comparison is a joy-killer. If you're looking, you can always find someone smarter, more successful, more attractive or more skilled than you. Instead, lean into God's plan for your life and become the best version of yourself. Thank Jesus for being perfect so that you don't have to be, and remember that in God's eyes, you are a masterpiece.

Lord, thank you for loving me even when I was your enemy. Thank you for offering mercy and grace so that I can be part of your family. Help me to walk in your plans with confidence and humility. Give me the ability to forgive myself when I make mistakes. Forgive me for comparing myself to others and help me to overcome any jealousy in my heart. Help me to encourage my brothers and sisters in Christ rather than competing with them. Help me to serve out of the overflow of your love as I fulfill the good things that you have planned for my life. In Jesus' Name, Amen.

Personal Reflection

As you go throughout your day today, take captive any self-deprecating thoughts and resist the tendency to compare yourself with others. Rather than beating yourself up for perceived flaws and mistakes, thank God for your gifts and talents.

_____

_____

_____

_____

_____

_____

_____

_____

_____

_____

_____

_____

Day 30
Smokey's Best Friend

Smokey has a best friend named Max. Max is also a mini-schnauzer, and he lives next door. Although Smokey and Max are separated by a fence, they love chasing each other back and forth along the property line. If Max is inside, Smokey will sit on high alert watching Max's door, waiting for his friend to come outside.

Unfortunately for Smokey and Max, their impulse to chase one another has not served them well. Max, who is much older than Smokey, broke several toes attempting to keep up with the younger dog. Smokey, who I've already told you is accident prone, gashed his shoulder open on a protruding nail head on two occasions. The lacerations resulted in sedation, stitches, and hefty vet bills. I would love to say that Smokey and Max learned from their mistakes, but I can't. They compulsively chase each other at every opportunity.

At least Smokey and Max have a good excuse for their behavior—they are animals who act on impulse and instinct. You and I, on the other hand, have the capacity for restraint. Paul tells us in Galatians 5:22–23 that patience and self-control are fruits of the Spirit. We are divinely empowered to refrain from any and every unwise course of action.

The author of Proverbs teaches us that self-control is even more beneficial than strength. He says, "Better to be patient than powerful; better to have self-control than to conquer a city," (Proverbs 16:32). When we live in a measured and thoughtful manner, we protect ourselves and the people we love. If we sprint through life relying on instinct and power, we often rush headlong into disaster. Smokey had plenty of strength and speed when he gashed his shoulder open on the fence, but we have divinely gifted faculties to avoid dangers in our path. Let's tap into the patience and self-control that the Spirit makes available. As much as I love animals, I'd rather not act like one!

Lord, thank you for providing self-control and patience so that I can make wise decisions. I repent of behaving rashly and allowing my impulses to control my actions. Help me to evaluate my instincts and bring them under submission to your Spirit. Help me grow in patience so that I learn to wait on your timing. Help me grow in self-control so that I can live wisely, avoid harm, and honor you. In Jesus' name, Amen.

Personal Reflection

Recall an occasion during which you acted rashly or spoke impulsively, and the outcome was strife or harm. How could you have handled the situation in a more productive manner? What can you learn from your mistakes that might help you react more thoughtfully and wisely in the future?

_____

_____

_____

_____

_____

_____

Day 31
Schnauzer Sounds

Mini schnauzers are characteristically loud. Their frequent vocalizations are both adorable and annoying. In their more irksome moments, Smokey and Pepper bark at every squirrel that passes our window and every guest that approaches our door. Alternately, their "woooo-wooooing" when we arrive home is the sweetest sound in the world. Pepper will even grab her ball in excitement and continue wooo-ing around a mouth full of tennis ball. Smokey, who is generally less vocal than Pepper, makes his own unique sounds. When relaxed, he groans like an old man, and when nervous, he whines like a squeaky toy.

Smokey and Pepper bark, snarl, and growl at each other too. Sometimes they bark playfully, and sometimes they snarl furiously. When frustrated, they both make a hilarious grumbling sound that I'm pretty sure is a combination of growling and cursing.

The sounds that Smokey and Pepper make are an indication of how they feel and what they want to communicate. Even without words, I can discern whether they are happy, angry, afraid, excited, relaxed or wary. I can tell if they want something, like food, or are simply guarding their territory. I can tell whether they are playing with each other or expressing frustration.

Words are important because they reveal our inner self. Through speech, we not only convey information, but we also express how we feel and what we want. The way we speak shows who we are and how we perceive the world. Our words declare our intentions, our dreams, our hurts, and our hang-ups.

Tomorrow, we'll talk more about the relationship between our words and our heart. Today, we'll begin building greater self-awareness about the connection between our words and our inner self. Use the following questions to help you evaluate your patterns of speech and the condition of your heart.

Do I listen more than I speak? James instructs us to be quick to hear and slow to speak (James 1:9). Are you listening to understand or just waiting until you can talk?

Do I feel the need to prove my point at all costs? Relationships are more important than being right. Just because something is true doesn't mean it needs to be said.

Are my words true? Sometimes hard truths need to be spoken. Even when the truth hurts, it can bring long-term healing. Conversely, deceptive or false words cause deep and lasting harm. According to Proverbs 25:18, "Telling lies about others is as harmful as hitting them with an ax."

What is the intention behind my words? Make sure that your words are delivered from a heart of love and respect. If you catch yourself speaking with the intent to manipulate harm, or deceive, you should hold your tongue and reconsider your words.

Do my words reflect emotional health and self-control? Be sure to think before you speak! We nearly always regret words spoken in anger or frustration.

Do my words bring hope? Seek to reflect the image of God by offering hope, encouragement, and life.

Lord, thank you for giving me the faculty to communicate clearly. Forgive me for speaking out of impure, selfish, or manipulative motives. Give me greater wisdom so that I will know when to speak and when to remain silent. Give me the discernment to know when encouragement is needed and when someone simply needs a listening ear. Purify my heart so that my words would emerge from a heart that is healed and whole. Help me to model patterns of speech that honor you and bring life to others. In Jesus' name, Amen.

Personal Reflection

As you meditate on your patterns of speech today, use the above questions to self-evaluate and redirect your words if necessary. Consider what the content of your speech says about the condition of your heart.

_____

_____

_____

_____

_____

_____

_____

_____

Day 32
Consider the Source

Words are important because they reveal the condition of our heart. Through speech, we convey information, we declare what we want, and we share our opinions. Our words also express how we feel, who we are, and how we perceive the world. James teaches that whatever is inside of our hearts will eventually come out of our mouths. "Does a spring of water bubble out with both fresh water and bitter water? Does a fig tree produce olives, or a grapevine produce figs? No, and you can't draw fresh water from a salty spring," (James 3:11–12).

James is pointing out that it is impossible for something of one kind to produce something of a completely different kind. A fig tree cannot bear olives. A grapevine can't produce figs. An apple tree can't grow bananas. A cat can't have puppies. A fish can't birth a frog. And a heart full of hate can't produce healing words.

I've told you before that I lived on a small farm as a child. Because we were far from city utilities, we dug a well behind our home. In theory, the well was going to provide all the water we needed. Unfortunately, the water was full of sulfur, and it stank like rotten eggs. No matter how much we wanted pure water, we weren't going to get it from that well. The source of the water was contaminated, and it was unusable.

In much the same way, our words reveal the true condition of our heart. Like water from a well, if bitterness pours from our mouth, we can deduce that the source of the water, our heart, is contaminated by bitterness. If manipulative, selfish, angry, or hateful words pour from our mouth, they expose a polluted heart. Conversely, speech that is loving, encouraging, and joyful flows from a heart that is pure and healthy.

Consider the source of your words today. Is your well sulfurous and stinky or pure and refreshing? There was no reasonable recourse for purifying our sulfur well, but you have the power of the Holy Spirit at your disposal.

Lord, thank you for creating a clean heart in me. I pray that you would help me guard against contaminants and pollution. Forgive me for speaking words from selfish and hurtful motives. Help me to recognize when my speech reflects impurities in my heart. Thank you for making me aware of hurtful patterns of speech and providing the means of cleansing through Christ. Guide me as I seek to become healthier in my heart so that I can speak words that reflect your character. In Jesus' name, Amen.

Personal Reflection

Continue growing in self-control by refraining from harmful words and seeking opportunities to offer grace. Today, in addition to verbal speech, consider the impact of your written communications through social media, text, and email.

_____

_____

_____

_____

_____

Day 33
New Mercies every Morning

In my younger years, I was a "morning person." Most days, I was up before five in the morning to study or exercise. Recently though, my internal clock has flipped. I tend to stay up late at night, and I despise getting up early. My husband, Wesley, is always awake before me, so he helps me get going. Wesley brews coffee, gets the dogs from the boys' rooms, and brings both to me in bed. Waking up to dog kisses and coffee makes me feel like a queen.

Wesley's kindness and faithfulness never cease to amaze me. Why does he serve me so lovingly each day? His love isn't because I cook delicious meals, because I keep a tidy house, or because I'm such a kind and compassionate wife. My domestic skills are passable at best. Wesley is loving and faithful simply because that is his nature. I haven't done anything to earn his love, yet he gives it freely.

Wesley's love helps me understand the love of my Heavenly Father. My Father has fresh blessings for me every single morning that are even better than coffee and dogs! The prophet Jeremiah tells us that "The faithful love of the Lord never ends! His mercies never cease. Great is his faithfulness; his mercies begin afresh each morning," (Lamentations 3:22–23). Your Father's gifts aren't based on your obedience or your service, but on his character. He blesses you, not because you are good, but because he is.

Although Jeremiah's words sound exuberantly joyful, the prophet actually delivered them to Judah during a period of exile and devastation. Whether you are in a season of rejoicing or a season of trial, God's mercy, grace, and love are available every morning. Your Heavenly Father knows exactly what you need for each day. But we still have to take hold of the gifts he offers. I could choose to ignore Wesley's daily gifts of coffee and dogs, but why would I? Let's turn our eyes to our loving Father and seize his fresh mercies every day!

Lord, thank you for offering me fresh mercies every morning. Thank you for providing enough grace to cover over every mistake and enough strength to withstand every trial. Thank you for loving me and filling my heart with joy. Help me develop a habit of seizing your mercies in the morning and taking them with me throughout my day. I repent of ignoring you and the blessings that you offer. Help me walk in your faithful love and remember that your grace is based on who you are rather than what I do. Open my eyes to opportunities to share your mercy, grace, and love with others. In Jesus' name, Amen.

Personal Reflection

Begin creating a habit of meditating on God's fresh mercies each morning. Instead of scrolling through your phone as soon as you awaken, spend a few minutes conversing with your Father. You may want to put a note on your mirror or bedside table as a reminder.

_____

_____

_____

_____

_____

Day 33

Day 34
The Pumpkin Story — Part 1

Since we are in the fall season, I thought I would share a funny pumpkin story. Well, it's funny now, not so much when it originally happened. One year during the fall, when Abel and Asher were around three and six years old, respectively, we went to the grocery store to get some items for dinner. As we proceeded through the produce section, they saw the pumpkins and desperately wanted to pick one out. Well, as a typical three-year-old, Abel hadn't been on his best behavior that day. So, I saw an opportunity. I told the boys that they could get a pumpkin if they promised to be very good. But I also told them that if they did not behave while we were in the store, I would put the pumpkin back.

Poor little three-year-old Abel just couldn't hold up his end of the bargain, and so as promised, I put his pumpkin back in the pumpkin bin. You can imagine that he wasn't very happy about that, and everyone in the store knew it.

I'll leave you on a cliff-hanger and finish the story tomorrow, but let's pause here for a moment. Clearly, I was trying to teach Abel good behavior through disciplinary action. He didn't enjoy it at all, but no one enjoys discipline. It is painful, and even embarrassing at times. The author of Hebrews explains this principle. "No discipline seems pleasant at the time, but painful. Later on, however, it produces a harvest of righteousness and peace for those who have been trained by it" (Hebrews 12:11).

Discipline is painful, but we need it for training in life. I disciplined Abel because I wanted him to learn better patterns of behavior. I want to equip him for a successful life, and sometimes that means correcting poor behavior with disciplinary measures. Our loving heavenly Father does the same. When his children act in ways that are damaging to themselves or others, God often takes steps to redirect behavior in a healthier direction. Although the discipline may be painful, it will yield a harvest of peace and righteousness. God isn't angry with you, but rather, desires to protect you and train you for a fruitful life.

Lord, thank you for being attentive to my life. Even though your discipline can be painful, I thank you for helping me walk in peace and righteousness. Help me respond to discipline in a way that honors you by correcting any behaviors that dishonor you or create harm. Help me to learn from my mistakes and your restorative guidance. In Jesus' name, Amen.

Personal Reflection

Sometimes God's discipline comes from external factors, and sometimes he allows us to suffer the consequences of our own actions. Either way, our response to his discipline determines whether we learn from our mistakes. Think of several circumstances in the past in which you have faced discipline. How did you respond? In what ways could you have responded more productively. What can you learn from your mistakes to help you more effectively navigate discipline in the future?

Day 35
The Pumpkin Story — Part 2

I left you on a cliff-hanger yesterday with Abel's pumpkin story, so let's pick up where we left off. Asher, Abel, and I were in the grocery store. Abel was screaming because he wanted a pumpkin that I refused to buy. He was causing quite a scene, so I decided to prematurely conclude our trip to the store, even though I wasn't finished shopping. So, we proceeded to the check-out lane, I loaded my few groceries onto the conveyor, got my wallet out of my purse, and put my debit card into the reader. As I looked up, the wide-eyed cashier said "Uh . . . ma'am?" and pointed to the exit. I looked up just in time to see Abel dart out of the automatic exit doors. He had jumped out of the cart and made a run for it. I didn't know what to do. I was standing there with my purse open, wallet out, and card in the reader. I couldn't just run off and leave. So, I turned to Asher, who looked like a deer in headlights. I said "Asher! Go grab Abel and keep him out of the street!" So, Asher dashed out, and I was seconds behind. Asher had managed to get a precarious hold on this apparently feral creature known as Abel. So, I dumped all my stuff and grabbed Abel. Asher picked up all my belongings and finally, blessedly, we were on the way to the car.

Sadly, this story isn't over. We arrived at the car. Asher got in and buckled himself. I, wrestling Abel with all the strength in my body, finally got him buckled into his car seat. With a massive sigh of relief, I got in the front seat, buckled myself, and turned on the car.

Thinking we were ready to go, I glanced in the rearview mirror. We were not ready to go. Abel had undone all the buckles on his car seat, and as I watched, opened the door and tore off across the parking lot, screaming the whole way. Asher and I jumped back out of the car, chased Abel around the parking lot, finally caught him, and wrestled him back to the car. It was clear that the car seat buckles would no longer hold Abel, so I crammed him into the car and told Asher to hold him down. I was able to engage the child door locks to prevent another escape, and we were finally on our way home. Fortunately, I didn't live too far from the store, and I have never been so relieved to pull into my driveway. I'm exhausted just *thinking* about this story. Yet, I will do anything to protect my children.

God, likewise, protects his children, and one facet of his protection is wisdom. The author of Proverbs advises, "Do not forsake wisdom, and she will protect you; love her, and she will watch over you," (Proverbs 4:6). God gives his children the faculty to employ wisdom, but we also have the option to reject prudence. How many times have you done something that you knew wasn't a good idea? How many times have you sensed God's divine guidance, yet chose to go your own way? I don't know about you, but I have ignored God's wisdom more times than I care to admit.

Like stubborn toddlers, we get angry with God because we want to have our own way. We run from him and lash out, when God is simply protecting us from danger. Just as I chased Abel through the parking lot and restrained him from going further, God establishes safe boundaries for our lives by providing wisdom. Just as Abel didn't understand why I was restraining him; we often don't understand the boundaries that God establishes (Isaiah 55:8–9). We don't need to understand everything, though, because we can trust that our Father wants the best for his children. According to Psalm 9:10, "Those who know you, Lord, will trust you; you do not abandon anyone who comes to you." Let's thank him for his constant care and protection, even when we try to go our own way.

Lord, thank you for being faithful, even when I turn from you. Thank you for leading me toward paths of wisdom, even when I am obstinate. Thank you for providing healthy boundaries, even when I don't like them. Help me always remember that your ways bring life and blessing. Thank you for loving me, redeeming me, and protecting me. Help me grow in my relationship with you to such an extent that my life is characterized by wise decisions and obedient faith. In Jesus' name, Amen.

Personal Reflection

Scripture repeatedly tells us that when we ask for wisdom, God provides. Strive to make a habit of asking God for wisdom in your daily prayer time and throughout each day. If you have time today, read Proverbs 3 and write down everything you learn about wisdom.

Scan the QR code for passages of Scripture

Day 36
Houseplants

I don't like being cold. Therefore, in the fall and winter, I bring nature inside with me. I conscript my boys into a day of work moving outdoor plants indoors. I place temporary shelving in the best lit rooms, and even set up plant lights to supplement the ambient light. All winter long, I water the plants regularly and prune away dead foliage. Nonetheless, they generally don't thrive. My outdoor plants can't thrive inside because they don't receive enough light.

Plants utilize photosynthesis to convert light into energy and nutrition. Despite my supplemental LED "grow lights," my indoor-outdoor plants do not get enough light for sufficient energy and food. Without enough energy and food, they can't grow and flourish. Fortunately, their sad, dormant state transitions into a thriving cycle of growth when they move back outdoors in the spring.

A new location, however, won't always remedy problems. If I move one of my permanent houseplants outside because it's failing to thrive, the leaves will get burned to a crisp in the sun. Simply shifting the plant to a different location doesn't fix the fundamental problem. Since houseplants enjoy low light, the unhealthy plant likely had the wrong amount of moisture or a lack of nutrients in the soil.

Sometimes we feel like a change of location will fix our problems. We try a new church, a new job, a new house, or even move to a new city. Yet, making a change for the wrong reasons will only exacerbate our problems. Before we alter external facets of life, we should make sure that our inner life is in balance.

Like plants, you and I need the right balance of nutrients to thrive; we need certain elements to maintain a healthy spiritual life. Luke provides a helpful survey in Acts 2 as he describes the activities of the early church. For the sake of space, I'll summarize. Members of the early church spent time in fellowship, prayer, worship, and Bible study. They stewarded their resources faithfully and served one another. Because they stewarded well and shared resources, they were able to minister to the poor in their community (Acts 2:42–47).

Although Acts 2 isn't written as a list of commands believers must follow, the activities of the early church provide a healthy model for us to follow. The spiritual nutrients that we need to thrive include prayer, Bible study, community, worship, stewardship, and service. Each element is vital for maintaining a healthy and balanced life of faith.

Lord, thank you for demonstrating a healthy life of faith while you lived upon this earth. Help me follow in your footsteps as I seek to develop a faith that honors you. I pray that my time in study, prayer, and worship would be nourishing and meaningful. I pray that my fellowship and stewardship would bless others as I am likewise edified. Please reveal any spiritual nutrients in which I am deficient. Give me greater discernment so that as I seek to synthesize healthy habits, I would simultaneously release any habits that detract from my growth. In Jesus' name, Amen.

Personal Reflection

Consider the list of spiritual nutrients: prayer, Bible study, community, worship, stewardship, and service. Does your spiritual life include each practice? If so, what adjustments can you make to create better balance between the different elements? If not, what steps can you take to implement one practice that you are lacking?

Day 36

Day 37
Sunburned Plants

Throughout the fall and winter, I look forward to weather that is warm enough to bring my outdoor plants back outside. They are a constant source of irritation for me because they appear sad and unhealthy. I know that when I get them back into the sunlight that they will become lush and beautiful again. I've learned, however, that I can't rush the process.

Did you know that plants can get sunburned? I learned about plant sunburn one spring when I gleefully moved my plants from the house into direct sunlight on the back patio. In only a couple of days, every plant appeared faded, scorched, and worse than before. I discovered that when a plant is moved from an area of low light into greater brightness, it must be acclimated a little at a time. The process is called "hardening" and is a bit like getting a base tan before you head to the beach. Hardening the plant involves exposing it to gentle light for short periods, and then gradually increasing the light intensity and length of exposure. As the process continues, the plant becomes stronger and more tolerant of bright sunlight.

As Christ followers, we also undergo seasons of preparation and strengthening similar to the hardening process. Although our Heavenly Father equips us with gifts, we must learn to use them in order to accomplish his calling. These seasons of preparation may be lengthy, tedious, and grueling, but God will move us to the next step when the time is exactly right. In Hebrews 10:36 we learn that "Patient endurance is what you need now, so that you will continue to do God's will. Then you will receive all that he has promised."

Becoming frustrated or trying to circumvent the equipping process can have disastrous results. We can harm ourselves or others and even derail the dreams that God has placed in our hearts. At the very least, our service might be less than effective because we have neglected to cultivate the right skills and character. We must steward our gifts, dreams, and seasons of equipping as precious treasures from God. When we patiently persevere and allow God to set the pace, our lives will bear fruit in just the right season.

Lord, thank you for the perfect plans you have for my future. Help me to trust in your timing and patiently endure the process of preparation. Grow my strength and resilience so that I can overcome any obstacle in my path. Equip me with the character and skills I need to fulfill your good plans for my life. Give me the wisdom to invest my time in pursuits that bear good returns for your Kingdom. In Jesus' name, Amen.

Personal Reflection

Meditate on what God might be equipping or preparing you for in the future. Consider how you can patiently grow during your present season so that you can attain the full measure of his plans and blessings for your future.

_____

_____

_____

_____

Day 38
Caught in the Net

Yesterday we talked about seasons of preparation and equipping for God's plan in our lives. During these seasons, we inevitably encounter trials, which seem to rise up and become a massive obstacle blocking the path forward. However, trials aren't a distraction from our preparation, but rather, part of the process.

Habakkuk was an Old Testament prophet who ministered to Judah during the period of Babylonian oppression. He cried out to the Lord on behalf of Judah, expressing anger and anguish over their oppression. Habakkuk asked the Lord, "Are we only fish to be caught and killed? Are we only sea creatures that have no leader? Must we be strung up on their hooks and caught in their nets while they rejoice and celebrate?" (Habakkuk 1:14–15). As Habakkuk petitioned God, the prophet struggled to understand why God was taking so long to rescue his people. Yet, the people of Judah had been behaving like capricious minnows and feral sea monsters long before they were set upon by Babylon. Although they had a powerful leader—Yahweh— they had neglected to follow him.

Nonetheless, God promised a future time in which he would vindicate his people. The Lord explained to Habakkuk, "This vision is for a future time. It describes the end, and it will be fulfilled. If it seems slow in coming, wait patiently, for it will surely take place. It will not be delayed," (Habakkuk 2:3). Judah was in a season of refining and repentance. God took no delight in the suffering of his people, but he allowed the trial to take place in order to change hearts. He used hardship to renew their faith and strengthen their resolve. Although the fickle hearts of God's people had been tossed about by the sea, God used Babylon to shore up their faith.

Seasons of preparation are just as much about attuning our hearts to God as they are about gaining skills and knowledge. Hopefully, your season of preparation will not be as brutal as that of Judah, but you will face trials. When you do, remember that you follow in the steps of many faithful saints, and even your Savior, Jesus Christ. The very trials that feel like a roadblock may actually be the preparation needed to propel you forward.

Lord, thank you for modeling a life of patience and faithfulness. Help me patiently navigate the process of preparation so that I'm ready at the right time. Help me to remain faithful and persevere through difficult seasons. Help me to view my trials and obstacles as opportunities to grow in faith and character. Equip me with the skills and knowledge I need to serve you fruitfully. In Jesus' name, Amen.

Personal Reflection

Think about any areas of your life that you view as a distraction from or detriment to God's plan for you. Reassess each situation and ask God what you can learn that will help you grow in faith, skill, or character.

_____

_____

_____

_____

Day 38

Day 39
Double Down

Yesterday, we discussed trusting God and persevering in the face of trials. Today, we'll let not-so-good king Ahaz show us how *not* to respond to trials. Ahaz ruled roughly 150 years prior to the ministry of Habakkuk, another period during which Judah faced enemies on every side. Second Chronicles 28 provides the account.

> *At that time King Ahaz of Judah asked the king of Assyria for help. The armies of Edom had again invaded Judah and taken captives.* **18** *And the Philistines had raided towns located in the foothills of Judah and in the Negev of Judah. They had already captured and occupied Beth-shemesh, Aijalon, Gederoth, Soco with its villages, Timnah with its villages, and Gimzo with its villages.*
>
> ### 2 Chronicles 28:16–18

Judean cities and villages were being invaded throughout the country. Judean citizens were being dragged from their homes and into slavery. With the threat of the Assyrian Empire looming on the horizon, Ahaz did as any logical ruler would do and sought an alliance. Assyria, with her formidable military might, would serve as a powerful ally and protector! Right? Wrong. Instead of helping Judah, Assyria attacked!

Have you ever made a decision that seemed wise in the moment, but actually made your situation worse? Your "logical" solution only added tinder to the fire. A bad situation became worse simply because you were trying to make a good decision. Why would God let this happen to his children? Let's return to Ahaz for an answer.

Instead of seeking God's help, Ahaz had orchestrated his own plan. Then, when his plan backfired, Ahaz obstinately shunned the Lord and "doubled down." He relied on his own logic, his own solutions, and his own strategies. We learn that "Even during this time of trouble, King Ahaz continued to reject the Lord," (2 Chronicles 28:22). Even worse, Ahaz sought aid from false gods.

> *He offered sacrifices to the gods of Damascus who had defeated him, for he said, "Since these gods helped the kings of Aram, they will help me, too, if I sacrifice to them." But instead, they led to his ruin and the ruin of all Judah. The king took the various articles from the Temple of God and broke them into pieces. He shut the doors of the Lord's Temple so that no one could worship there, and he set up altars to pagan gods in every corner of Jerusalem. He made pagan shrines in all the towns of Judah for offering sacrifices to other gods. In this way, he aroused the anger of the Lord, the God of his ancestors.*

2 Chronicles 28:23–25

All of Ahaz's planning and plotting utterly failed. The defeated king left a scant legacy other than faithlessness and failure. His only positive contribution to the world was his son, Hezekiah, who was righteous despite the example of his father.

I know Ahaz is not an admirable figure, but I believe we can learn from him. When we rely on our own solutions, we exacerbate our problems. Yet, if we humble ourselves and turn to the Lord, he is always ready to defend and protect. He is the most powerful ally available, and even better, he knows us, loves us, and protects us. Let's not double down on our mistakes, but rather double back to seek the guidance of the Lord.

Lord, I acknowledge your power and love. Thank you for standing at the ready to defend me when I call. I repent of attempting to solve problems without your guidance. Help me rely on you and not on my own plans and purposes. Gently remind me to turn to you for guidance and direction in every situation. I pray that I would bring light and restoration to my world as I live in the center of your will. In Jesus' name, Amen.

Personal Reflection

Meditate on your response to personal mistakes. Do you struggle to admit fault? Are you quick to seek guidance and direction from your Heavenly Father or do you try to concoct solutions on your own?

_____

_____

_____

_____

_____

_____

Day 39

Day 40
Playing Opossum — Part 1

The opossum is the only marsupial native to North America. Though many people consider them repugnant, opossums are quite underappreciated. As expert scavengers, they eat ticks, slugs, roaches, and even small rodents. Opossums keep their environment clean by consuming virtually any type of dead animal, and they keep their environment safe by consuming venomous snakes.

Their behavior around predators is the source of the phrase "playing possum." When threatened, opossums roll onto their back, bare their teeth, drool saliva, and excrete a foul-smelling substance. They even slow their breathing to an imperceptible degree. Their instinctive behavior serves to trick predators into thinking they're dead. Since most predators prefer live prey, the apparent death of the opossum confuses the predator enough to seek a different meal.

Whether you love them or hate them, you can learn several lessons from opossums. Lesson one, opossums make their environment better. They aren't afraid to do the dirty jobs that no one else wants. Lesson two, opossums utilize the slim resources at their disposal to survive against unfavorable odds. They aren't fast, they don't see well, and they are literally paralyzed by fear. Although they have the ability to climb well and swim quickly, they prefer to amble on the ground. Opossums clearly aren't the cleverest animals in the forest, yet they are resilient and resourceful. Lesson 3, after facing a life-threatening trial, they get back up and keep lumbering along.

The apostle Paul embodied these principles throughout his ministry. He worked tirelessly and made the world better by spreading the Gospel of Christ. He was ridiculed, beaten, stoned, and arrested, yet got back up after every beating. Even when imprisoned, Paul exhibited resilience and resourcefulness by writing letters and ministering through intermediaries. In 2 Corinthians 4:8–9, Paul professes, "We are pressed on every side by troubles, but we are not crushed. We are perplexed, but not driven to despair. We are hunted down, but never abandoned by God. We get knocked down, but we are not destroyed."

Like the opossum, Paul epitomized resilience and resourcefulness. Even during his own suffering, he offered encouragement, joy, and hope. He chose to press through hardships rather than crumple beneath them. He viewed his trials as opportunities and praised God in every circumstance. We'll talk more about that tomorrow, but for today, let's work on lesson one and make the world a better place. How can you positively impact your surroundings today?

Lord, thank you for Paul's encouraging model of service, resilience, and resourcefulness. Help me to utilize the resources you have placed at my disposal to make the world around me better. Give me the strength to persevere through every situation that seems hopeless or feels like defeat. Provide opportunities for me to serve in ways that others might find distasteful so that I can grow in resilience. Thank you for helping me become more like Jesus through my service and sacrifice. In Jesus' name, Amen.

Personal Reflection

As you go through your day, seek opportunities to serve others by completing tasks that are undesirable or neglected. You will benefit by growing in resilience and your peers will be blessed by your service.

Day 41
Playing Opossum — Part 2

Yesterday, we talked about opossums, the most misunderstood and underappreciated marsupials. Their distinctive defense mechanism, feigning death, helps them survive against predators. Opossums aren't particularly agile or cunning, but they are extraordinarily resilient and resourceful. Although they literally fall over in fearful or stressful situations, they always get up and get on with life.

The prophet Micah probably never saw an opossum, but he understood resilience. Micah ministered to Judah during the reigns of several kings, one of whom was Ahaz. Do you remember Ahaz—the faithless king who doubled down on his mistakes? Ahaz was a wicked king and an abysmal leader. He literally dismantled and smashed the sacred items inside the temple, then locked the doors so that no one could worship in the sanctuary (2 Chronicles 28:24). Ahaz was such an abominable person that he sacrificed his own children to pagan gods (2 Chronicles 28:3).

Utter depravity was the spiritual climate into which Micah was called for ministry. God tasked Micah with speaking against the pervasive evil in Judah, and the prophet obeyed. Micah boldly declared, "Listen to me, you leaders of Israel! You hate justice and twist all that is right. You are building Jerusalem on a foundation of murder and corruption," (Micah 3:9–10). Scripture gives little indication of how his message was received, but Micah himself may offer one hint. He wrote, "Do not gloat over me, my enemies! For though I fall, I will rise again. Though I sit in darkness, the Lord will be my light," (Micah 7:8). More than likely, Micah spent time inside a dark prison cell. He was almost certainly ridiculed, rejected, and physically abused by his own people. Yet, no amount of resistance prevented Micah from delivering the Lord's message and fulfilling his calling. Micah prophesied boldly and even angrily at times, but he never grew bitter. Even as he spoke words of rebuke, the prophet offered a hopeful message. Although Judah would be ravaged, brutalized, and exiled, she would rise again.

Just as God equipped Micah with resilience, he will provide for you. You may get knocked down; you may be ridiculed, rejected, and abused; but you will get up again. Just like Micah, just like Paul, and just like those opossums, you'll use the resources God has provided for you, and you will survive. Even better, through God's love, you will thrive.

Lord, thank you for providing everything I need to accomplish your calling and live an abundant life. Help me grow in resilience so that I can more effectively serve you. I repent of being angry with you when I face disappointment, rejection, or abuse. I believe that you have a good plan for my life and that you have equipped me to overcome every trial. Give me the discernment to identify the resources you have provided and the wisdom to utilize them effectively. In Jesus' name, Amen.

Personal Reflection

Meditate on your past responses to rejection, disappointment, and hardship. When knocked down, do you get back up and get on with life or do you spiral into despair? Do you seek joy or settle into despondency? Do you retreat into isolation or seek support from the community in which God has placed you? Take some time to evaluate your past, then look toward the future. What resources, strengths, and skills has God placed at your disposal? How can you become more resilient and efficient with your God-given resources?

_____

_____

_____

_____

_____

_____

_____

_____

_____

_____

_____

_____

_____

_____

Day 42

Seriously? Another Opossum Devotional?

Yes, we are still talking about opossums. I never would have guessed that they are such interesting and inspiring creatures, at least in their own special way. After extolling their virtues for the last two days, I would like to point out a behavior that we should not emulate, namely freezing up in the face of danger.

When threatened, the opossum enters a state called thanatosis and appears to be dead. As most predators prefer live prey, they will abandon the seemingly dead carcass. Though this instinct can protect the opossum from harm, the paralysis also endangers it. During thanatosis, the opossum remains unconscious and immobile with no control over its mind or body. This catatonic state can last for up to four hours, leaving the opossum utterly defenseless. While the marsupial is vulnerable, more intelligent predators have ample opportunity to eat or kill the poor opossum.

Primary threats to the opossum include humans and owls. Humans, often mistakenly believing that opossums are rodents, will take action to eliminate the unwanted creature. Alternately, some people enjoy eating opossum and claim that the meat tastes similar to lamb. (Ewww—no thank you!) Owls are also a major opossum predator. Although owls aren't scavengers, they occasionally eat dead animals and aren't always deterred by the opossum's fake death.

What I want you to understand is that holding onto victimhood places you in a vulnerable position. If we allow it, our victimhood will become our identity. We'll continue to embrace it because it feels safe and familiar. Sometimes we even take subconscious pride in our status as a victim because we receive special attention and sympathy. At the same time, holding tight to our victimhood forces us to relive our trauma over and over again. We continue to think and act in ways that may have once kept us safe, but that now prevent us from becoming whole. Clinging to our status as a victim prevents us from moving forward with life because we are stuck in the past. Even worse, perpetually identifying as a victim increases the likelihood that we will allow people to treat us as a victim and hurt us again.

I want to stress that we should never be ashamed of trauma in our past, and we should celebrate individuals who overcome abuse. At the same time, we shouldn't embrace an identity of victimhood.

In our culture, victimhood is increasingly becoming a virtue. More and more often, people assume the mantle of a victim based on perceived slights and imagined offenses. Instead of becoming stronger and healthier, they become more fragile and dysfunctional because they build a catalog of reasons to be angry and unhappy.

A victim mentality stands in direct contradiction to the teaching of Scripture. Through Christ, we are victors, not victims. Even when Paul was imprisoned, he claimed victory. In Philippians 1:12–14, he rejoiced that "everything that has happened to me here has helped to spread the Good News. For everyone here, including the whole palace guard, knows that I am in chains because of Christ. And because of my imprisonment, most of the believers here have gained confidence and boldly speak God's message without fear."

Instead of viewing himself as a victim, Paul recognized the opportunities and blessings by which he was surrounded. When we fix our gaze on Christ, it's impossible to fix our gaze on trauma. Let's follow the example of Paul's life and the wisdom of his teaching, "Be thankful in all circumstances, for this is God's will for you who belong to Christ Jesus," (1 Thessalonians 5:18).

Lord, thank you for accepting unimaginable abuse, ridicule, and rejection in order to defeat sin, sickness, and death. Thank you for saving me and transforming me from a victim into a victor. I trust that you will take every situation that the enemy intended for harm and use it to accomplish your good purposes. Teach me to be thankful in every circumstance and help me see opportunities instead of offenses. In Jesus' name, Amen.

Personal Reflection

Throughout your day today, immerse your mind in gratitude. If you find your thoughts drifting toward trauma, ask God to redirect your thoughts toward opportunities for victory. If you catch your mind dwelling on a grievance or offense, begin to express gratitude for your blessings.

_____

_____

_____

_____

_____

_____

_____

_____

Day 42

Day 43

Good King Hezekiah

Over the last few days, we have been talking mostly about opossums. The odd little marsupials teach us about resilience and resourcefulness, but they also demonstrate how we should not respond to trials. When faced with danger, the opossum becomes paralyzed. While this instinct functions as a defense mechanism, it also places the opossum in danger.

Behaving and thinking like a victim is dangerous for both opossums and humans. Yesterday, we talked about why a victim mentality is harmful, and we read about Paul's shining example of optimism. Today, I would like to bring your attention to another biblical figure from whom we can learn.

Hezekiah was a Judean king who had every reason to identify as a victim. Hezekiah was the son of Ahaz—the same Ahaz who dismantled the temple and sacrificed his sons. Apparently, Hezekiah was one of the lucky sons who didn't get murdered as an infant. When he grew up and succeeded his father as king, Hezekiah inherited a people who rejected God and a country who faced the threat of Assyrian domination. Instead of following the example of his father, Hezekiah sought God and prayed for guidance. In fact, he served God more fervently than any Judean king that preceded or followed him (2 Kings 18:5).

Hezekiah was the direct opposite of his father. When Assyria marched on Jerusalem, Hezekiah entered the temple and prayed for help, unlike Ahaz, who had locked and barred the temple (2 Kings 19;

2 Chronicles 28:24). Because Hezekiah was faithful, God miraculously delivered Jerusalem, causing the majority of the Assyrian soldiers to die in their sleep and the remainder to flee in fear.

Later in Hezekiah's reign, the king again employed fierce resilience. Hezekiah grew deathly ill, such that God spoke through the prophet Isaiah and instructed Hezekiah to get his affairs in order and prepare for death (2 Kings 20:1). "When Hezekiah heard this, he turned his face to the wall and prayed to the Lord, "Remember, O Lord, how I have always been faithful to you and have served you single-mindedly, always doing what pleases you." Then he broke down and wept bitterly. But before Isaiah had left the middle courtyard, this message came to him from the Lord: "Go back to Hezekiah, the leader of my people. Tell him, 'This is what the Lord, the God of your ancestor David, says: I have heard your prayer and seen your tears. I will heal you, and three days from now you will get out of bed and go to the Temple of the Lord," (2 Kings 20:2–5).

Hezekiah had ample reason to adopt a victim mentality. His father, Ahaz, was a malevolent king who murdered Hezekiah's siblings. When Hezekiah grew into adulthood, he inherited a kingdom near ruin. Hezekiah faced the threat of Assyria, a temple that had been ransacked, and a nation full of idolaters. Yet, he led the people back to the Lord with a firm hand and resolved each problem with God's help.

Hezekiah had no control over his parentage, his father's corruption, the apostasy of his people, or the aggression of Assyria. Hezekiah did, however, have a choice about how he would respond to each situation. Rather than giving up, pining for sympathy, or using trauma as an excuse for destructive behavior, Hezekiah employed resilience and resourcefulness. Even when Hezekiah's resilience was exhausted and his body near death, he used the one resource that remained available. Hezekiah cried out to God and prayed so fervently that God miraculously healed him.

Like Hezekiah, you may face trauma that is beyond your control. Although you can't always control your circumstances, you can definitely choose how you will respond.

Lord, thank you for equipping me to persevere through trials and trauma. Give me the wisdom to recognize the resources you put at my disposal and use each one effectively. Fill me with joy even when my external circumstances are joyless. Fill me with gratitude even when I inherit a multitude of problems. Teach me to respond to offense with grace as I follow the example of my Savior, Jesus. Help me be more intentional about acknowledging my blessings and seizing opportunities to express gratitude. In Jesus' name, Amen.

Personal Reflection

Today, when you encounter opportunities for frustration or offense, remember that you have a choice about how you will respond. Practice responding with resilience and kindness. Once again, if you catch your mind dwelling on a grievance or offense, begin to express gratitude for your blessings.

_____

_____

_____

_____

_____

Day 43

Day 44
Hezekiah's Hubris

Hezekiah was a good king, but he wasn't perfect. His success made him complacent, and his riches made him proud. The arrogance in his heart led to the greatest mistake of his life, which took place shortly after God's miraculous healing.

When the king of Babylon had heard that Hezekiah was ill, he sent envoys with get-well gifts. At that time, Babylon's power was rising, so for Hezekiah to receive an envoy from the Babylonian king was a great honor. Isaiah explains, "Hezekiah was delighted with the Babylonian envoys and showed them everything in his treasure-houses—the silver, the gold, the spices, and the aromatic oils. He also took them to see his armory and showed them everything in his royal treasuries! There was nothing in his palace or kingdom that Hezekiah did not show them," (Isaiah 39:2). King Hezekiah wanted to impress his guests, and he gave them the royal tour.

At first glance, Hezekiah's actions don't seem all that bad. However, we find out from 2 Chronicles 32:24–30 that Hezekiah struggled with pride. God had blessed Hezekiah with success and riches, and the king's heart had become proud. Hezekiah's heart was so prideful that it blinded him to the threat Babylon represented. He was so arrogant that he couldn't see the ulterior motives of the envoys, who were surveilling Judah for their king.

Hezekiah epitomized the saying "proud as a peacock." Whether or not peacocks actually have the mental capacity for arrogance, they certainly appear proud of their beauty. The flamboyant bird will lift his feathers, fan his plumage out for maximum visibility, and quiver his iridescent feathers in order to catch the light. He'll then strut in slow circles so admirers can gaze upon his beauty. In a similar fashion, Hezekiah strutted around and showed off his riches. Instead of treating the envoys with discretion, arrayed the full glory of Judah before Babylon.

Unfortunately for the peacock, his feathers attract more than admiration. His bright plumage draws the attention of predators. Like the splendor of the peacock, Hezekiah's riches became the source of his destruction. I have to wonder if Hezekiah had ever heard the familiar proverb, "Pride goes before destruction, and haughtiness before a fall," (Proverb 16:18). With his gratuitous display of wealth, Hezekiah made Judah a desirable target for Babylon. His hubris set in motion a chain of events that lead to the fall of Judah and the subjugation of her people.

That which seems to be our most beautiful treasure or most valuable asset can turn into our greatest weakness. If we aren't careful, pride will cause us to fall more in love with ourselves and our treasures than God. Instead of acknowledging that everything we have is from him, we begin to believe that our treasures come from our own efforts. We take credit instead of thanking God, and eventually we begin to live as though we don't need him at all. We slip into a subtle idolatry in which we worship ourselves, our accomplishments, and our riches.

Instead of allowing pride to take root and wreak destruction in our lives, we can cultivate humility and gratitude. When we humbly acknowledge that every gift is from God, we inoculate ourselves against arrogance. Even better, God can continue to bless us because we steward his gifts well. Let's thank God at every opportunity!

Lord, thank you for blessing me with resources, skills, and gifts. Forgive me for neglecting to acknowledge that everything I have comes from you.

Help me stay so full of gratitude that pride has no room in my heart. When I'm tempted to think or act arrogantly, please renew a spirit of humility in me. Help me always guard against pride so that I can live within your protection and blessing. In Jesus' name, Amen.

Personal Reflection

Spend another day focusing intently on gratitude. As you navigate your day using the skills and resources God has provided, express gratitude for each. When you make mistakes or notice your own shortcomings, thank God for helping you remain humble.

_____

_____

_____

_____

_____

_____

_____

_____

_____

_____

Day 45

Opossum Party

Have you ever heard of an "opossum party"? I hadn't until I recently began reading about opossum behavior. Apparently, a possum party entails staying awake all night and eating junk. Another version of the possum party involves climbing a tree in the middle of the night, getting drunk, and then trying to climb down without getting injured. I don't recommend either version of the possum party, especially the latter. I've never taken part in a possum party, but I've done plenty of things that were just as irresponsible and hazardous to my health.

As Christ followers, we are often careless with our physical health even when we are devoted to growing in spiritual health. However, the spirit, soul, and body are intricately related. If we abuse or neglect our physical bodies, our mental and spiritual health will also suffer. Our bodies are a gift from God and a resource that belongs to him. As such, we should steward them with care. Furthermore, when we steward our physical body wisely, we are better equipped to grow in spiritual wellness, serve God faithfully, and fulfill his purpose for our lives.

Everyone is aware that an unhealthy diet or lack of physical activity creates a downward spiral of declining health. However, many people don't realize that regular patterns of sleep and rest are just as crucial. Rest is so important that God commanded his people to observe a day of rest each week. As one of the Ten Commandments, taking a day of rest was a distinguishing characteristic that set Israel apart from her neighbors (Exodus 20:8–11). For an agrarian society in which survival depended on one's labor, taking an entire day to rest each week was a sign of great faith in God's provision. The practice of sabbath rest was continued into the New Testament era. Although layers of legalism had accrued around the observance, Jesus described the sabbath as a blessing from God, not simply a command to be obeyed (Mark 2:27–28).

Similar to rest, sleep is regarded as a gift from God throughout Scripture. Sleep is frequently associated with peace (Psalm 4:8), provision (Psalm 127:2), and protection (Psalm 3:5). According to Ecclesiastes, sound sleep is a reward for hard work (Ecclesiastes 5:12).

Although sleep is a blissful reward, it is also vital for our health. Sleep is required for the body to flush the brain of toxins that can lead to neurodegenerative diseases like Alzheimer's. Other maladies caused by lack of sleep include emotional instability, depression, memory impairment, and diminished capacity for logical thought. Long term sleep deprivation can even cause permanent damage to the brain. Alternately, healthy sleep patterns boost the immune system, reduce the potential for heart problems, and improve productivity.

Opossums were designed to stay up all night and eat garbage. Even so, most don't live past their first year, and the oldest opossum on record only lived to the age of four. Unlike the opossum, humans are created in God's image and are called to a higher purpose. As such, our wellness requires greater care. So, turn off the television, put up the junk food, get off your phone, and get some rest!

Lord, thank you for providing opportunities for rest and refreshing in my life. Help me trust you enough to take advantage of them. Give me the self-discipline to steward my body well so that I can serve you better. Help me make wise choices in regard to my physical activity, eating habits and patterns of rest. Forgive me for neglecting my physical health and guide me toward wellness in every area of life. Help me exemplify good stewardship, efficient service, and steadfast faith. In Jesus' name, Amen.

Personal Reflection

Pray and meditate on your own patterns of sleep and rest. Do you routinely get enough sleep or are you perennially sleep deprived? Do you reserve a period of time each week for sabbath rest and intimacy with God? Evaluate your schedule and seek God's guidance about any changes you might need to make.

Day 46
Opossum Imposter

Did you know that there is a difference between an opossum and a possum? Although the words sound the same, the breeds are quite different. The species found in North America, the one we have been discussing, is the Virginia opossum. A different type of marsupial is found throughout Australia, New Zealand, and New Guinea. These overseas cousins resemble the Virginia opossum and were thus named "possum" due to physical similarities.

Nonetheless, significant differences distinguish the possum from the opossum. Most notably, the Australian marsupials do not exhibit the defense mechanism of feigning death. In appearance, they have a fluffy tail, as opposed to the hairless, rat-like tail of the Virginia opossum. The faces of the Australian possum are less pointy, and their fur is golden-brown. In regard to diet, the Australian possum is much more refined, preferring to eat only plants instead of garbage and carcasses. In effect, the Australian marsupials are significantly more appealing in appearance and behavior.

Despite the differences, most people have difficulty telling the species apart. I would warrant a guess that most people don't even realize that the opossum and possum are two different creatures.

In Scripture, we find another case of mistaken identity, one that is far more sinister. Several passages reveal that Satan, and his minions strategically emulate Christ. Paul warns, "Even Satan disguises himself as an angel of light. So, it is no wonder that his servants also disguise themselves as servants of righteousness," (2 Corinthians 11:14–15).

The author of Revelation, with true apocalyptic flair, describes a beast from the earth who looks like a lamb but speaks like a dragon. In other words, the beast appears spiritual, but his words are lies. This land beast colludes with a beast from the sea who mimics Christ's resurrection by recovering from a fatal wound. Although the beasts pretend to be holy, their spiritual veneer hides a deceptive and evil intent.

The objective of our Enemy is to steal, kill, and destroy (John 10:10). Yet, he hides his true intention behind shallow spirituality and deceptive delights. The Enemy persuades us to fulfill our base desires and worship a false god of self-indulgence. He promotes a tawdry version of love that encourages us to celebrate every vice and flaw. He convinces us to applaud people for "living their best life" as they careen toward destruction. The Enemy promises joy and fulfillment but delivers is pain and strife.

Christ doesn't offer false assurances of a fairytale life. Our savior shows us that true love involves sacrifice. His love isn't about telling people what they want to hear but confronting destructive behavior. If we love like Christ, we are willing to risk rejection for speaking the truth. Living our best life actually involves following Christ through trials instead of jumping ship or numbing ourselves with distractions.

We must remain diligent and guard against deception. The lies of the enemy are persuasive, but he has already been defeated by Christ. While we walk in wariness, we also walk in wisdom and victory. If we keep our eyes on our Savior, we will be equipped to spot imposters from a mile away.

Lord, thank you for offering life-giving truth. I repent of being tempted by the lies of the enemy. Give me greater discernment so that I can recognize his deception without hesitation. Help me to model sacrificial love, even when speaking the truth is hard. Give me the strength to stand strong in my faith, even when my beliefs are not popular. I confess that I don't understand all of your ways, but I trust that you are the only way, truth, and life. In Jesus' name, Amen.

Personal Reflection

Today, simply raise your awareness of the enemy's strategies. Watch for thoughts, conversations, and behaviors that appear to be spiritual or loving, but are actually shallow and false. Evaluate yourself as well as your environment in the light of Scripture. When you notice deceptions, remind yourself of God's truth.

_____

_____

_____

_____

_____

_____

_____

_____

_____

_____

_____

Day 46

Day 47

Opossums and Lions

North American opossums are solitary creatures. Their only social behaviors are mating and caring for babies. Most other interactions are characterized by aggression or apathy. For example, they're violently territorial even though they don't occupy a fixed territory. I can't help but wonder if they might live longer than one year if they banded together and helped each other out.

Many species of animals benefit from communal behaviors. Lions, for example, live together in groups, or "prides." When the pride needs food, the females leave the group to hunt together, while the males remain behind to protect the pride. The females stay together as they hunt so that if they encounter a large animal, they can work together to catch their prey. If a female lion is harmed and unable to care for her cubs, the other females will protect and nurture the young lions.

Community is a principle built into the fabric of God's creation. Because God designed us to live in community, we are more healthy, successful, resilient, and joyful when we do life together. The author of Hebrews exhorts, "Let us think of ways to motivate one another to acts of love and good works. And let us not neglect our meeting together, as some people do, but encourage one another, especially now that the day of his return is drawing near," (Hebrews 10:24–25).

From these verses, we can deduce that creating healthy community requires intentionality. We should not only think about ways to encourage one another but take action to support the people in our lives. We should not only prioritize communal worship and fellowship but schedule it into the fabric of our lives. Anything meaningful requires time and effort, and community is no exception.

While opossums have some admirable traits, their social skills leave much to be desired. Let's learn from the example of the lion pride. With the all-powerful Lion of Judah leading our pride, we are guaranteed to thrive.

Lord, thank you for establishing your church on this earth. I repent of neglecting my faith family. Forgive me for ignoring the needs of your church and your Kingdom. Bring to my attention ways that I can encourage and motivate my brothers and sisters in Christ. Help me manage my time wisely and prioritize gathering with my community of faith. I eagerly look forward to the day when you return to gather your people to spend eternity with you. In Jesus' name, Amen.

Personal Reflection

Foster a habit of seeking opportunities to encourage members of your faith family. You can mail a kind note, deliver a meal, or call someone and pray for them. If you are extra motivated, you might consider visiting someone who is lonely, babysitting for a single mom, or secretly meeting a financial need in your church.

_____

_____

_____

_____

_____

Day 48
Purple Passion

Purple passion is the common name of a gorgeous, leafy, shade plant. Its leaves are dark green, but they're covered in tiny purple hairs, giving the plant a velvety, iridescent appearance. It is relatively easy to grow in pots indoors or in shady areas outdoors. The downside to purple passion is the plant's propensity to attract whiteflies.

Last summer, I had a purple passion living on my patio. I knew it had whiteflies and I wanted them gone before the plant came inside for winter. So, I planned to give it a thorough dose of neem oil. Neem oil is a naturally occurring pesticide that repels bugs and kills larvae. It is non-toxic for humans and is even used in some cosmetics and skin medications, although it should not be ingested.

Armed with my bottle of neem, I began to douse the plant. After several liberal sprays, I noticed that my bug killer smelled like bleach. Upon looking at the label, I realized that I had, indeed, sprayed bleach on my plant. Immediately, I turned on the water hose and rinsed the plant as thoroughly as possible. I didn't follow up with neem oil because I thought the bleach certainly would have killed any pests. I watched the plant closely for several days, hoping I hadn't inadvertently killed it. Fortunately, the plant continued to thrive. Unfortunately, so did the whiteflies.

The whiteflies survived because I never sprayed the plant with neem oil. Because I didn't complete the process, I merely got rid of a few bugs who were sitting on the surface of the leaves. The eggs, which are glued to the underside of the leaves, remained intact. In less than two weeks, I had a whole new crop of whiteflies swarming over the leaves. We'll talk more about the whiteflies tomorrow, but let me pause here to make a point.

Often when we begin to follow Jesus, we feel so joyful about our commitment that we expect our lives to change dramatically. Maybe we've had a profound encounter with God, during which we sense his presence in an almost tangible way. By his grace, we receive cleansing and a new outlook on life. Yet, we must continue to take steps toward a changed life. If we simply enter into a relationship with Christ, yet never take another step forward, our old patterns of thought and behavior will reemerge, just like those whiteflies.

The apostle Paul guided the earliest Christians to spiritual maturity. He advised the Ephesian believers to "Get rid of all bitterness, rage, anger, harsh words, and slander, as well as all types of evil behavior. Instead, be kind to each other, tenderhearted, forgiving one another, just as God through Christ has forgiven you," (Ephesians 4:31–32).

When we begin walking with Jesus, we are a little like my purple passion, crawling with bugs of bitterness, anger, unforgiveness, and all the baggage that we have accumulated throughout life. Christ washes us clean with his love and grace, but if we mistakenly believe that the process is complete, we are sorely mistaken. In Philippians 1:6, Paul exclaims, "I am certain that God, who began the good work within you, will continue his work until it is finally finished on the day when Christ Jesus returns." When we accept Christ, he becomes not only our Savior, but our Sanctifier who helps us grow. He teaches us to replace bitterness with kindness, anger with forgiveness, and hate with love. If we allow Jesus to continually cover us with his love and shelter us with his grace, those little bugs will no longer find a home in our heart.

Lord, thank you for helping me replace bitterness, anger, slander, and evil behavior with kindness, forgiveness, and love. When my former actions and reactions rise to the surface, help me turn to you for cleansing. Give me the desire to grow in sanctification and the discipline to follow you. Give me a passion for growing in holiness so that I can help others experience your cleansing and salvation. In Jesus' name, Amen.

Personal Reflection

Today, be mindful of patterns of speech or behavior that don't reflect your salvation and sanctification. When you notice one of those "bugs" making an appearance, be intentional about squashing it. Prayerfully seek the help of your sanctifier to continue his process of cleansing in your heart.

_____

_____

_____

_____

_____

_____

_____

_____

_____

Day 49

Bad Company

Yesterday we talked about my purple passion plants and my efforts to rid them of the whitefly infestation. In addition to being a nasty insect that I don't want inside my house, whiteflies literally suck the life from plants. They have long, needle-like mouths with which they pierce plants and extract sap. The bugs then excrete a sticky substance that causes mold and fungus. Adding insult to injury, whiteflies don't remain confined to one plant. They will reconnoiter the area for other delicious plants upon which they can dine.

Whiteflies are similar to the pests that cause crepe myrtle bark scale and are likewise notoriously hard to exterminate. As I mentioned yesterday, even spraying bleach on my purple passion didn't kill the bugs. I'm not a quitter, though, so I continued my war against the repulsive little bugs. With my bare hands, I picked off each tiny whitefly and whitefly nymph (wingless baby whitefly). Even so, they were back within a week. To protect my other plants, I had no choice but to get rid of the infested purple passion.

You and I can also become infected if we aren't careful—not by whiteflies, but by bad character. Our friend Paul warns, "bad company corrupts good character," (1 Corinthians 15:33b). We talked about the importance of cultivating relationships in a previous devotional. I want to emphasize that finding *healthy* relationships is vital. Paul cautions that close association with "bad company" is even worse than being alone. An unhealthy community, like a swarm of whiteflies, will suck the life out of you and corrupt everything in your vicinity.

With both plants and people, the best course of action is to take preemptive steps. Don't buy a plant with whiteflies, and don't form close connections with toxic people. Both will corrupt your life and spread dysfunction like a virus.

Let me be clear that you and I are called to love everyone, including people of questionable character. However, people who don't share our values are not going to be part of our inner circle of friends, mentors, and confidants. We can go to the plant nursery, browse the plants, and even sit down for coffee. We just don't take a diseased plant home and make it our best friend.

Lord, thank you for giving me the discernment to identify harmful influences. Help me exercise wisdom regarding my close friends and mentors. Reveal whether I should distance myself from any people in my life right now. Give me the courage to stand firm on my faith so that I can be a light to those who don't know you. Give me the strength to resist compromise even when I'm in the presence of people who live contrary to your Word. In Jesus' name, Amen.

Personal Reflection

Think about your inner circle of friends. Do the people closest to you help you draw closer to God or does being around them draw you further from him? Do you act more like Christ or less like him when you are around your friends? Ask God to reveal any relationships that are causing damage instead of growth. Ask God to show you how you can start distancing yourself from harmful influences.

Day 50
Going in Circles

Ecclesiastes is a peculiar book of Scripture. Of all 66 biblical books, Ecclesiastes is one of the most difficult to understand. The style of the book could be described as rambling, cynical, depressing, confusing, and even carnal. At the same time, one could describe the tone of the book as practical, hopeful, and thoughtful. Let me explain.

The author of Ecclesiastes, who identifies himself as "The Teacher," and whom tradition identifies as Solomon, systematically experiences everything under the sun. He samples everything that life has to offer—the good, the bad, and the ugly. He finally comes to the conclusion that every pursuit in life is meaningless. In chapter 1, he offers these bleak words:

> *The wind blows south, and then turns north. Around and around it goes, blowing in circles. Rivers run into the sea, but the sea is never full. Then the water returns again to the rivers and flows out again to the sea. Everything is wearisome beyond description. No matter how much we see, we are never satisfied. No matter how much we hear, we are not content.*

> ### *Ecclesiastes 1:6–8*

Our teacher concludes that everything is meaningless! Every pursuit is as pointless as wind blowing in circles. We are born, we live a miserable life, and then we die. Solomon does, however, offer a ray of hope later in the book.

Even so, I have noticed one thing, at least, that is good. It is good for people to eat, drink, and enjoy their work under the sun during the short life God has given them, and to accept their lot in life. And it is a good thing to receive wealth from God and the good health to enjoy it. To enjoy your work and accept your lot in life—this is indeed a gift from God. God keeps such people so busy enjoying life that they take no time to brood over the past.

Ecclesiastes 5:18–20

Maybe life isn't meaningless after all! Consider what we can learn from Solomon. First, he is teaching that despite trials and difficult seasons, the simple things in life can always bring us joy. We can enjoy a good meal with family or friends. We can take satisfaction in working productively. We can plant a garden, take a walk, or go for a swim. Second, our wise teacher proclaims that although life is short, we can take joy in living each day to the fullest. Life isn't perfect, but our teacher reminds us that God gives us good gifts. God wants us to enjoy his presence and provision afresh each day. Third, when we take delight in the simple joys of life and focus on God's good gifts, we will be too busy enjoying life to ruminate over what is wrong with our lives. In the original Hebrew, Ecclesiastes 5:20 literally says that God keeps us busy with joy! Even if we feel like we are going in circles, we can have fun while we do it!

Lord, I pray that you help me see the abundance of blessings in my life. Help me to take joy in your daily gifts, whether large or small. Help me to be more aware of your blessings than my trials. I pray that you would keep me so busy with joy that no trial could disrupt my gratitude or shake my faith. In Jesus' name, Amen.

Personal Reflection

Take some time right now to list some simple things that bring you joy, then express gratitude to your Father. As you go through your day today, be intentional about thanking God for simple blessings that bring you joy.

_____

_____

_____

_____

_____

_____

_____

_____

_____

_____

_____

_____

_____

Day 51

Carpe Diem

Let's spend another day in Ecclesiastes and look at a verse that is especially relevant during a global pandemic and its aftermath. Many people long for a time when we can "get back to normal" and "go back to the way things used to be." However, Solomon warns against this type of thinking. He advises, "Do not say, "Why were the old days better than these?" For it is not wise to ask such questions," (Ecclesiastes 7:10). Only God knows whether our lives will ever go back to "normal."

Let me share an illustration. When my family moved into our current home, Abel, who was five at the time, seriously missed our old house. It was the home in which he had lived his entire life, and in his five-year-old imagination, everything about that old house had been better than our new one. In reality, our new home was newer, nicer, and larger than our old home. Abel occupied a bigger bedroom and bathroom and acquired an entire playroom that he shared with his brother. Our new neighborhood even had a park and a pool, neither of which were available in our previous community. Clearly, Abel was seeing our old house through the lens of fond memories rather than reality. Nonetheless, he truly believed that our old home was better, and would periodically ask, "Why did we have to move?" and "Why can't we go back to our old house?" He couldn't enjoy the good things about our new house because he was so fixated on the old one.

I believe this is what Solomon is trying to convey in the verse above. God knows that if I am pining over "the good ol' days" and fixing my gaze on the past, I won't see the blessings of today. Remember, God has fresh mercies every morning (Lamentations 3:23). Instead of wishing for the past or worrying about the future, let's fix our eyes on Jesus and thank him for the blessings that he is showering upon us today.

Lord, thank you for blessing me in every season of life. Help me enjoy happy memories without longing for the past. Forgive me for giving more attention to my complaints than your blessings. Open my eyes to see the fresh mercies and opportunities you offer me each day. In Jesus' name, Amen.

Personal Reflection

Each season of life brings its own challenges and its own blessings. Take some time and think about what sparks joy in your current season. Thank God for each blessing.

_____

_____

_____

_____

_____

_____

_____

Day 52
Larger than Life

As humans, we understand the power of nature. Although the natural world prompts awe and at times fear, our mental framework readily accommodates what we can see, hear, and touch. We are appalled at the damage that natural disasters can wreak. We are astounded by complex ecosystems like rainforests. We are fascinated by the depths of the sea and the peaks of the mountains.

When we try to grasp the vastness of the universe, the scope just doesn't compute. Our solar system is over seven billion miles wide, and more than 500 solar systems populate the Milky Way alone! I don't know about you, but my mind doesn't have a framework for something that large. Even more difficult to conceptualize, our God created every galaxy, star, and planet.

The Psalmist offers many reflections on the vastness and power of our God. In Psalm 89, he exclaims,

O Lord God of Heaven's Armies!
Where is there anyone as mighty as you, O Lord?
You are entirely faithful.
You rule the oceans.
You subdue their storm-tossed waves.
You crushed the great sea monster.
You scattered your enemies with your mighty arm.
The heavens are yours, and the earth is yours;

everything in the world is yours—you created it all.
Psalm 89:8–11

Our God created the earth, the mountains, the seas, and the vastness of the universe. We can't quite wrap our heads around a universe so large or a being so powerful. Our finite minds simply can't process God's true nature.

Our solution, subconsciously, is to shrink God down to a more manageable size. As a result of worshiping this small God, our faith is also small. We have difficulty trusting him because he isn't much wiser or stronger than we are. We pray small prayers because we worship an anemic God. In effect, we create a God in our own image rather than coming to terms with the cognitive difficulty caused by his immensity. We must accept the fact that God is infinitely more mighty and infinitely more powerful than we can comprehend. According to Job 5:9, "He does great things too marvelous to understand."

Yet, our God is also more faithful than we can imagine. In verse 8 above, the Psalmist reminds us that God is "entirely faithful." Rather than confounding us, the Psalmist seeks to encourage us. The creator of the universe will defend us with all the resources of heaven and earth at his disposal. Instead of shrinking our faith, God's immensity should give us faith on steroids! So, even if we can't quite wrap our minds around God, our hearts can have peace knowing our Father is faithful to his children.

Lord, thank you for your faithfulness to me. I acknowledge that you are mighty enough to provide for me and protect me in every situation. Forgive me for having small faith and praying small prayers. Help me grow in faith and overcome my doubts. Help me rest in your power, provision, and protection today. In Jesus' name, Amen.

Personal Reflection

Meditate on your own faith. Do you have robust faith in the true, omnipotent God of the universe or do you have meager faith in an emaciated version of him. Do you make decisions based on trust in your Father or do you make decisions based on your fear and scarcity of resources? Challenge yourself to take one step of faith today.

_____

_____

_____

_____

_____

_____

_____

_____

_____

_____

_____

_____

_____

_____

_____

Day 53
Peacock Problem

Our family loves going to the zoo, and we especially love opportunities to interact with the animals. On our first trip to the Cincinnati Zoo, Asher was a toddler small enough to ride in a stroller. His only memory of the entire day is our encounter with the peacocks. To be honest, it's about the only thing I remember, too. For me, it was hilarious, but for Asher, it was horrible.

Until 2010, the Cincinnati Zoo had a large number of peacocks who were allowed to roam the property freely. The birds were so happy and healthy that their flock, or "ostentation," reproduced and grew rapidly. By 2010, the peacock population had swelled to 40, and the zoo was forced to rehome the large ostentation. Officially, the reason for rehoming the peacocks was their rapid breeding and overpopulation. I believe an additional factor was at play.

Our peacock encounter took place in 2009, at the height of the peacock population. Well accustomed to humans and secure in their numbers, the fowl had become quite aggressive. The peacocks, apparently, had learned that they could procure food from humans. And they liked it.

Halfway through the morning of our visit, we decided to have a snack. As soon as we sat down, the peacocks started closing in. I was delighted to be in close proximity to the beautiful birds. Asher was understandably wary because the birds were larger than he was.

Taking our snacks out of the bag, I deposited a few goldfish crackers on Asher's stroller tray. He scarcely had the opportunity to

177

grab one before the peacocks darted in to steal snacks for themselves. Asher's feelings toward peacocks immediately changed from wariness to animosity. He grew more and more angry and screamed more loudly each time a peacock snatched a goldfish.

I wish I could say that I rescued Asher from his distress by chasing the birds away, but that isn't what happened. Being the compassionate mother that I am, I continued placing goldfish on Asher's tray for the peacocks. Seeing a flock of huge, majestic birds stealing goldfish crackers from a toddler was more entertaining than I can describe. Eventually, my motherly instincts kicked in, and I saved Asher from the hungry birds. Although the whole encounter only lasted a few minutes, the memory will live in our hearts forever.

Let's think about how you and I respond to unexpected or frustrating situations. Hopefully, we don't scream and cry like a toddler, yet we often let our emotions run wild. When our emotions take over, everything we experience passes through the filter of what we feel. If we are angry, the smallest slight will make us angrier. If we are frustrated, every snag becomes more frustrating. If we are depressed, every interaction feels more disheartening. With such intensified emotions, we begin to act irrationally and make bad choices.

If we can keep our emotions in check, however, we'll retain the capacity to think clearly. Often, we see a solution or resolution before the situation has an opportunity to worsen. Even if we don't find a solution, remaining calm allows us to see God, access his strength, and abide in his peace. According to Psalm 46:1, "God is our refuge and strength, always ready to help in times of trouble."

As a toddler, Asher didn't have the mental and emotional capacity to stay calm. He was too upset to realize that I had plenty of goldfish for him and for the peacocks. He was too intimidated by their size to notice that his mother was bigger than the birds and plenty strong enough to protect him.

Unlike toddlers, you have the faculty to respond calmly under pressure. It does take practice, but you'll have plenty of opportunities. Next time a peacock gets in your face, look up at your Father, acknowledge his strength, and settle into his protective care.

Lord, thank you for being my source of strength and my place of refuge. Help me remember to focus on you when my emotions begin to overwhelm me. I acknowledge that my feelings can be misleading and distracting, and I repent of allowing them to control me in moments of stress. Help me to see the world through the filter of your love and peace so that I respond to every situation with wisdom and grace. In Jesus' name, Amen.

Personal Reflection

Make a conscious choice to submit your emotions to God today. In particular, give attention to the way you react to frustrating or stressful situations. When your emotions begin to rise, pause for a moment to breathe deeply and pray. Before you respond, ask yourself if you are responding through the filter of your emotion or through the filter of God's love.

Day 53

Day 54
Rico Suave

I can't mention the Cincinnati Zoo without telling you about Rico. Rico is a Brazilian porcupine, and he is the most adorable animal on Earth. I first "met" Rico during the covid quarantine. Since no one could visit in person, the Cincinnati Zoo began hosting "home safaris." In each home safari, the zoo staff featured a different animal. Zookeepers would discuss behaviors and traits while feeding or training the animal(s).

As I mentioned, Rico was my favorite. He has a soft pink nose, a long curly tail, and dexterous little hands. Although he is covered in sharp quills, he loves to be petted by his handlers. He also loves to eat banana chips, salad greens, dried fruit, and just about any crunchy produce. A favorite treat of Rico's is peanut butter. He'll hold a spoon in his little hands and methodically eat every drop.

A fun fact that I learned about Rico and other Brazilian porcupines is that they exude a distinctive smell. According to the zookeepers, the scent is a combination of onions and body odor. Initially, I assumed the smell would be subtle. At least, the trainers didn't seem to be bothered by it.

When the quarantine eventually ended, I was ready to meet Rico in person. As I have family who live less than an hour from the Cincinnati Zoo, we planned a trip to see family and visit the zoo together.

Fast-forward to our day at the zoo. I was beside myself with excitement as we approached Rico's enclosure. Before we could even see Rico, however, my boys asked, "What is that smell?" I knew instantly that it was Rico. From 10–15 feet away, through the glass enclosure, we could smell the little porcupine. His scent was not, in fact, subtle, but potent and pungent.

While you and I would consider Rico's smell offensive, it actually serves to protect him. The pungent odor is quite ominous for enemies of the porcupine. Predators recognize that the unique smell is associated with danger, i.e., sharp quills, and give porcupines a wide berth.

When I think about Rico, I'm reminded that no one is perfect. He is pleasant, but prickly, adorable, yet stinky. Just as we all have admirable qualities, we all have qualities that are not so appealing. We have our own strengths, and we have our own weaknesses. But like Rico's predator-repelling scent, Paul teaches that our weaknesses can become a source of strength. When Paul asked Jesus to take away his own weakness, the Lord replied:

> *"My grace is all you need. My power works best in weakness." So now I am glad to boast about my weaknesses, so that the power of Christ can work through me. That's why I take pleasure in my weaknesses, and in the insults, hardships, persecutions, and troubles that I suffer for Christ. For when I am weak, then I am strong.*

2 Corinthians 12:9–10

When we acknowledge our weaknesses and submit them to Christ, he transforms them. As we acknowledge our shortcomings, we simultaneously recognize our need for God. The recognition of our need for God prompts us to draw upon his power and surrender to his plan. What begins as a weakness can become a strength!

Before we left the zoo that day, I found a shirt in the gift shop that said, "Be more like Rico." I was thrilled to purchase the memento, and I wear it all the time. I'm not sure what the phrase is supposed to mean, but for me, it's an encouraging reminder. I don't have to be ashamed of my stinkier side because God can use even my worst traits for his glory. My flaws keep me humble so that I can be a vessel of God's power. Let's all "Be more like Rico" today.

Lord, thank you for working powerfully in and through my flaws. Thank you for helping me remain humble so that I'm not tempted by pride. Help me recognize my own weaknesses so that I am dependent upon your strength. Thank you for loving me despite my flaws, for loving me just as I am, and also for helping me grow in character. Increase my faith so that when I encounter struggles, I'm not discouraged, but rather encouraged because I see your powerful hand at work. In Jesus' name, Amen.

Personal Reflection

Consider your own weaknesses. Do you struggle with fear, anxiety, unforgiveness, or anger? Do you have a physical illness or ailment? Do you worry about situations beyond your control? Do you struggle with relational friction or workplace tension? Do you doubt that God is really powerful enough to protect and provide? Take some time right now to make a list of your five stinkiest struggles. Pray over each situation one at a time. Submit each struggle to God and ask him how you can glorify him in each situation.

_____

_____

_____

Day 54

Day 55
The Porcupine Predicament

Yesterday we talked about Rico, the adorable Brazilian porcupine. Rico reminds us that our weaknesses can actually be strengths. Today, we'll talk about Rico's North American cousins, who remind us that our weaknesses can be . . . weaknesses.

Like Rico, nearly all porcupines in North and South America are arboreal. The creatures live in trees and navigate the canopy with their long prehensile tails—at least most of them do. Out of 16 different tree porcupine species, only the North American ones lack a specialized tail.

The lack of a prehensile tail is problematic for the North American porcupine. Without the long tail, they simply aren't well suited for dwelling in trees. The stocky creatures have short arms and short legs. They can grow up to three feet long and weigh up to forty pounds. Although porcupines are talented climbers, the lack of a prehensile tail makes their balance precarious. I mean, if you look at pictures, the poor critters just look like they are about to fall out of their trees.

Unfortunately, falling from trees is exactly what happens. From time to time they'll tumble down to the forest floor. For an animal covered in quills, a fall spells disaster. They literally impale themselves on their quills! Fortunately, the punctures aren't usually fatal.

The weaknesses that you and I have typically aren't fatal either, but they can wreak havoc in our lives. If we submit our weaknesses to God and lean into his strength, he will fortify and protect us. If, however, we allow our weaknesses to draw us away from God, we step out of his protection and into danger.

When the people of Israel escaped from Egypt and moved toward the Promised Land, they routinely demonstrated fear over faith. Despite God's continued protection and provision, they failed to trust him. At the very borders of the Promised Land to which God had safely delivered Israel, they allowed doubt to derail their blessing. When the spies returned from advance scouting in Canaan, they lamented, "'We can't go up against them! They are stronger than we are!' So they spread this bad report about the land among the Israelites: 'The land we traveled through and explored will devour anyone who goes to live there. All the people we saw were huge'" (Numbers 13:31b–32).

The people of Israel had allowed their fears to become bigger than their God. In their weakness and fear, they could have turned to God and become an instrument of his power. Instead, they turned from God, stepped out of his protection, and faced dire consequences.

Those clumsy North American porcupines don't have the good sense to stay out of trees. When they fall, no one is going to catch them, and they'll face the consequences of their quills. We'll talk more about consequences tomorrow, but for now, remember that God's heart is to protect you, not punish you. If you leap out of God's arms, he might let you face those consequences. But he will always help you get back up and into his arms.

Lord, thank you for forgiving every weakness and shortcoming I have. Help me be aware of my weaknesses so that I can submit them to you and lean into your strength. Forgive me for trying to solve problems in my own strength. Give me the spiritual maturity to resist the temptation to go my own way in the future. Grow my faith and empower to obey you faithfully.

As my faith grows, I pray that my doubt would disappear in the light of your protection and provision. In Jesus' name, Amen.

Personal Reflection

Continue submitting your weaknesses and struggles to God today. Meditate on how you have handled your weaknesses in the past. Is your tendency to trust God or find your own ways to overcome your struggles? Do your past responses indicate that your heart is more filled with faith or doubt? Consider each "stinky struggle" you wrote down yesterday. Make a new list today and write down how you can trust God to strengthen you through each struggle.

_____

_____

_____

_____

_____

_____

_____

_____

_____

_____

_____

_____

Day 55

Day 56
Wilderness Wandering

The last couple of days, we've been talking about strengths and weaknesses. Our weaknesses can help us submit to God, draw closer to him, grow in faith, and become a vessel for his power. However, if we fail to entrust our weaknesses to God, they can lead to disastrous consequences. When the people of Israel failed to trust God and enter the Promised Land, they faced forty years of wandering in the wilderness. Even as he punished them, however, God was protecting his people. Let's look at how God responded to their failure.

The people of Israel had just escaped 400 years of slavery in Egypt. They had emerged from a polytheistic, pagan society and would soon enter a similar socio-religious context. When Israel balked at entering the Promised Land, they revealed that they weren't spiritually equipped to face the land's inhabitants. They hadn't yet learned to trust and obey God, and were therefore vulnerable to pagan influence.

God knew that his people needed his strength. To trust in his strength, they needed to experience his presence. God, in his foresight, had already made a way to dwell in the midst of his people in the form of the tabernacle. The tabernacle was a place where the people could safely meet with God and where he could meet with them. As Israel wandered through the wilderness, God went with them every step of the way.

Most people view the God of the Old Testament as angry, vengeful, and wrathful. We are much more comfortable with New Testament Jesus—our faithful, forgiving friend. But Jesus came to show us what God is like. Just as God tabernacled in the midst of Israel, Jesus tabernacled among us (John 1:14). Just as God taught Israel to live among polytheistic pagans, Jesus taught us how to live amidst people who don't know him. Our Lord does not change (James 1:17).

So how does God respond to our weaknesses, failures, and doubts? He meets us there, helps us grow, and helps us become stronger. Even if our actions incur consequences, God stays with us at every turn. He walks with us through every struggle and takes our strikes upon his own back. God doesn't kick you when you are down, he helps you up and protects you. Knowing we have a Father who loves us so unconditionally should inspire faith that is just as limitless.

Lord, thank you for your unfailing, unconditional love. Help me to grasp the depth of your love and trust you more. Grow my understanding of your grace and forgiveness so that I seek to obey you out of love rather than fear. Give me the discipline to spend time in your presence every day and the desire to know you more. In Jesus' name, Amen.

Personal Reflection

Pray over the lists you created the last two days. Confess your faith over each situation. Thank God in advance for transforming each weakness, struggle, or failure into a strength. Confess your love for your Savior and thank him for his unconditional love toward you.

_____

_____

_____

_____

Day 57
Life and Limb

Yesterday, we talked about God's response to your weaknesses. Today, we'll talk about how you and I should respond to our own faults, specifically areas of sin and disobedience. But first, let's talk about lizards.

Lizards have an unusual ability called autotomy. When under duress, they can amputate their own tail as a defense mechanism. In some species of lizards, the tail detaches only when physical stress is placed upon it. For example, if a predator catches the lizard by its tail, the lizard will detach the appendage and keep running. Other lizard species, such as geckos, can spontaneously throw their tails. In many species of lizard, the tail will continue to wiggle after amputation, distracting predators and giving the lizard an opportunity to escape.

This amputational ability makes me think of Matthew 5:29–30. Jesus warns, "So if your eye—even your good eye—causes you to lust, gouge it out and throw away. It is better for you to lose one part of your body than for your whole body to be thrown into hell. And if your hand—even your stronger hand—causes you to sin, cut it off and throw it away." Jesus advises us to take swift and decisive action against sin in our lives.

Why does Jesus use such strong language about sin? Hasn't he already forgiven us? Certainly, Jesus forgives every fault and failure. At the same time, he knows that if we use grace as a license to sin, it will lead to our destruction.

Solomon was one of the most wise and successful kings ever to rule Israel. Yet, his personal weaknesses destroyed his relationship with God and ultimately led to the division of his kingdom. We learn from 1 Kings that Solomon had a weakness for women.

> *Now King Solomon loved many foreign women. Besides Pharaoh's daughter, he married women from Moab, Ammon, Edom, Sidon, and from among the Hittites. The Lord had clearly instructed the people of Israel, "You must not marry them, because they will turn your hearts to their gods." Yet Solomon insisted on loving them anyway. He had 700 wives of royal birth and 300 concubines. And in fact, they did turn his heart away from the Lord. In Solomon's old age, they turned his heart to worship other gods instead of being completely faithful to the Lord his God, as his father, David, had been.*

> ### 1 Kings 11:1–4

Since Solomon refused to amputate the sin from his life, God had to remove the kingdom from Solomon's family line.

> *The Lord was very angry with Solomon, for his heart had turned away from the Lord, the God of Israel, who had appeared to him twice. He had warned Solomon specifically about worshiping other gods, but Solomon did not listen to the Lord's command. So now the Lord said to him, "Since you have not kept my covenant and have disobeyed my decrees, I will surely tear the kingdom away from you and give it to one of your servants.*

> ### 1 Kings 11:9–11

Even though the Lord had personally appeared to Solomon, the king turned away from him. Solomon built shrines to pagan gods and worshiped with his wives. Solomon's apostasy led to a vicious revolt during the reign of his son, the fracturing of the kingdom, and a downward slide of morality that continued for twenty years after Solomon's death. What a tragic legacy!

Jesus warns us because he wants to protect us. Our relationship with him isn't just about getting forgiveness and escaping damnation. Jesus wants to provide an abundant life! Unfortunately, the enemy is actively working to destroy God's good plan (John 10:10). Our sin is like a cancer, eating away at all the good work God is doing in our life. Like the tail of a lizard, cut it off and run!

Lord, thank you for teaching me the danger of tolerating sin in my life. Thank you for forgiving me and providing a path to healing. Give me the courage, strength, and self-discipline to cut away any sins of which I am aware. Give me the wisdom and discernment to recognize even subtle patterns of wrong thinking and behavior. I pray that you would open my eyes to the harmful consequences of sin. Help me always choose to follow your lead instead of going my own way. In Jesus' name, Amen.

Personal Reflection

Continue to pray over the lists you created the last several days. Ask God to show you if any of your struggles are sin related. Ask God to show you if amputation is needed in any area. Ask God to show you where swift and decisive action might be required. As you pray, remember that your Savior wants to protect you, not condemn you.

Day 58
Lizard Lessons

Until the last decade, lizards were considered asocial. Recent studies, however, have demonstrated that lizard relationships might be more complex than we previously assumed. For example, in a study performed on chameleons at the University of Sydney, early social experiences appeared to have a considerable impact on adult behaviors. Chameleons raised in isolation appeared to be weaker, both in the ability to secure a mate and forage for food. A much larger lizard, the crocodile, also exhibits social behaviors. Mother crocodiles were long thought to cannibalize their young. However, more recent studies have shown that the mothers hold their babies in their mouths to protect them until they can fend for themselves.

Our social and familial interactions help us become who God created us to be. No one, neither human, animal, nor reptile grows to maturity in complete isolation. Sometimes we learn how NOT to act from negative influences. More often though, close friends and mentors help us navigate life with wisdom and grace.

Two proverbs are especially appropriate. First, Proverbs 19:20 instructs, "Get all the advice and instruction you can, so you will be wise the rest of your life." In other words, be proactive about asking for advice. Second, the author of Proverbs tells us, "As iron sharpens iron, so a friend sharpens a friend," (Proverbs 27:17). If we have the right kind of friends, they'll help us grow into God's purpose and plan.

In fact, the friends and mentors that God places in our lives are often the means by which he helps us mature.

Lord, thank you for placing people in my life who can help me grow. Help me be authentic and transparent as I interact with my friends and mentors. Give me the humility to confess my faults and failures to other people. Help me be more proactive in seeking wise counsel and allowing trusted mentors to speak wisdom into my life. In Jesus' name, Amen.

Personal Reflection

Your reading for today was short because your personal reflection is more substantial. Revisit your list of struggles one final time. Prayerfully choose one friend or mentor with whom you can share your list. Reach out today and ask them to partner with you in praying over each struggle. Give them permission to provide accountability regarding any patterns of thinking or behavior that need to change.

_____

_____

_____

_____

_____

_____

_____

_____

Day 59
Toad-ally Horrible

I've told you before that I love to learn. All my life, I've taken delight in exploring nature and learning about God's creatures. At one point when I was around five years old, I became very interested in toads and frogs. I was so curious that I wanted to know what they looked like on the inside, so I took action to satisfy my curiosity. I went outside, caught a toad, and found a sharp rock with which to dissect him.

I'll just stop the story right there and tell you that my experiment didn't go well. I've felt horrible about that undertaking for my entire life. Although my intent wasn't malicious, my lack of forethought and empathy caused great harm to an innocent creature. I'm embarrassed and ashamed of my actions.

Most of us find it difficult to acknowledge the harm that we cause. We rarely acknowledge our own faults but find it easy to point out flaws in others. We are slow to ask forgiveness, but quick to accuse our offenders. We loudly vent our own wounded emotions but accuse others of overreacting.

We all exhibit some level of double standard when it comes to hurt and offense. When we acknowledge that we have made a mistake, we make ourselves vulnerable. Because we put our weakness on display, we lose relational status. Because we relinquish some of our power, we place ourselves at the mercy of another.

The instinct for self-preservation doesn't mean that we're evil. It simply means that we are human. As humans, we are flawed and imperfect. We make mistakes. We hurt the ones we love. We kill help-less toads. (Lord, forgive me!)

Our Father is already aware of our flaws and failures. In fact, he teaches us how to overcome them. In 1 John 1, we learn that "If we claim we have no sin, we are only fooling ourselves and not living in the truth. But if we confess our sins to him, he is faithful and just to forgive us our sins and to cleanse us from all wickedness. If we claim we have not sinned, we are calling God a liar and showing that his word has no place in our hearts," (1 John 1:8–10). The first step in an authentic relationship with God is acknowledging our sin. When we recognize our own faults and repent of them, we can take steps toward avoiding mistakes in the future. When we turn away from sin and turn toward God, he equips us to fulfill the greatest command in Scrip-ture—loving God and loving our neighbors (Matthew 25:35–40).

If we truly seek to embody God's love and extend it to others, we must be willing to acknowledge our weaknesses and humble our-selves. Part of that process is thinking through our actions, consider-ing the impact of our words, and learning to live compassionately. When kindness becomes our default response, reconciled relation-ships will replace grudges and encouraging interactions will replace an-gry accusations.

I've made so many hurtful mistakes. I regret words that caused pain. I regret the times I sought revenge. I regret retaliating in anger. I regret hurting that toad. Yet, that same regret helps me move forward. I'm learning from my mistakes, and I won't make the same ones again. How about you?

Lord, I confess that I have caused hurt and pain. Forgive me for being careless with my words. Forgive me for lashing out in anger. Forgive me for being apathetic to the impact my actions might cause. Help me learn from my mistakes so that I don't repeat them. Bring to my attention any patterns of speech or behavior that might be hurtful to others. Help me to seek reconciliation instead of retaliation. Allow me to see your children through your eyes and love people with your heart. In Jesus' name, Amen.

Personal Reflection

Ask God to help you honestly self-reflect on your response to your own mistakes. Do you readily admit fault or search for something/someone else to blame? Do you ask for forgiveness or rationalize hurtful behaviors? Do you seek peaceful solutions or retaliate in anger? Acknowledge your faults to God and ask him to make your heart more sensitive to the impact of your words and actions.

Day 60
Sourpuss

Since we are talking about shameful actions in my past, let me tell you about Sourpuss the cat. The incident with Sourpuss took place around the same time as my experiment with the frog. At that time, I lived out in the country on a small farm with cows, chickens, goats, horses, dogs, and cats.

Farm cats are a bit different than house cats. They aren't pets as much as they are workers. They live in the barn and contribute to the farm by eating rodents that they catch and kill. It's a win for everyone. The cats are happy, and the farm is pest-free.

Since barn cats roam freely, they also procreate freely. As a result, kittens were always cropping up, which was delightful for me, my sister, and our cousins. Each time a litter was born, we would search out the tiny kitties to make sure that they were well cared for.

We knew that cats didn't like water, but we couldn't understand why. We absolutely loved playing in our kiddie pool, in the creek, in swimming pools, and any other body of water. We reasoned that cats would be safer and happier if they could simply learn to swim. We expected that once they learned, they would love the water as much as we did. Thus, as enterprising country-girls, we resolved to teach our favorite kitten to swim.

To prepare for our swim lesson, we donned swimsuits, filled our kiddie pool with water, and located the kitten henceforth known as Sourpuss. As we expected, the kitten offered considerable resistance, but our resolve was firm. We held the poor cat in the water until she stopped resisting, not realizing that we were actually drowning her.

Only by the grace of God and the kindness of my mother was the kitten spared from certain death. Using the sixth sense that only mothers have, my mom rushed to the scene and rescued the poor kitten. She literally provided mouth to mouth resuscitation and chest compressions to save the cat's life.

After that day, Sourpuss was never quite "right." I don't know whether she had emotional scarring or brain damage or both. Regardless, she never liked humans, and would hiss at anyone who tried to approach. Although we tried to make amends with treats and affection, she offered nothing but claws and teeth.

I'm legitimately ashamed of what we did to Sourpuss, but I share it because I think we can learn an important lesson from my mistake. You and I can't force anyone to behave a certain way just because we think they should. We may genuinely want to help them and have valuable lessons to impart. However, if they don't want what we are offering, pressing the issue becomes counterproductive. We'll end up wasting our own time and possibly even harming the one we're trying to help.

The author of proverbs talks about the effectiveness of unwanted guidance. He teaches, "A proverb in the mouth of a fool is as useless as a paralyzed leg," (Proverbs 26:7). Put another way, we could say that giving wisdom to someone who doesn't want it is as useless as forcing a cat to swim. Neither will yield the desired results.

Only God can prepare hearts for change and growth. The most effective strategy we can employ is to pray for the individuals we want to help. Only after seeking God's guidance should we proceed and offer wisdom or guidance. Even then, we can only offer love, support, and resources. Let's do our part and let God do his.

Lord, thank you for providing me with opportunities to serve people in my life and help them grow. Help me know when to speak and when to remain silent. Give me discernment to know when someone I care for is ready to receive guidance. Speak through me as I seek to impart your wisdom to others. Help me to never point out flaws or weaknesses in others for the purpose of condemnation. Help me to humbly recognize my own weaknesses and continue to grow as I serve those around me. Help me remember that it's your job to change hearts while I minister obediently under your direction. In Jesus' name, Amen.

Personal Reflection

How do you proceed when you see others making bad choices or when you feel like you have helpful wisdom to impart? Are you overly aggressive or passive? Do you pray and seek God's direction before you speak, or do you launch missiles of wisdom at everyone around you? Do you tell people what they want to hear, or do you speak the truth in love as needed? Ask God to show you how you can develop a more mature and measured approach to helping others grow.

_____

_____

_____

_____

_____

_____

_____

Day 61

A Good Reputation

In Western culture, owls have a reputation for being highly intelligent. The stereotype of the wise owl reaches all the way back to ancient Greece. Athena, the Greek goddess of wisdom, was symbolized by the owl, which by association gained a reputation for having great knowledge and perception.

In reality, owls exhibit subpar intelligence. Since most owls have large eyes and mouths, not much skull space is available for their brains. They are exceptional hunters, but they simply aren't that smart compared to other birds. For example, parrots can speak, jackdaws can count, and crows can construct and utilize tools. Owls, on the other hand, routinely fail simple cognitive tests like pulling a string to get a treat.

Unfortunately, reputation doesn't always align with reality. In Revelation 3, Jesus exposes the false reputation of the church in Sardis. He says, "I know all the things you do, and that you have a reputation for being alive—but you are dead," (Revelation 3:1b). Jesus warns that he will come against the church "suddenly, as unexpected as a thief" for the purpose of judgment (Revelation 3:3b).

As with the church of Sardis, Jesus' harshest rebukes in Scripture are directed toward religious people. He isn't impressed by a good reputation or noteworthy credentials. For example, Jesus criticized the Pharisees, calling them "whitewashed tombs" (Matthew

23:27). Their reputation was pristine, but they were deathly ill on the inside. Similarly, Paul has little compassion for people who pretend to live righteously, calling them detestable, disobedient, and worthless (Titus 1:16). Ouch!

Are you more interested in reputation or righteousness? Are you more concerned with keeping up appearances or keeping your heart pure? Living for Jesus is very different than pretending to live for Jesus. When we pretend to live for Jesus, we are more interested in our reputation than our relationship with him. Instead of acknowledging faults, we cover them up. Instead of seeking healing, we pretend everything is perfect. When we live for Jesus, we acknowledge our faults and failures. We routinely express repentance, pursue his grace, and seek the approval of our Savior.

I'm sure that you want to live for Jesus, but it's easy to slip into reputation maintenance mode. When you are tempted to whitewash your flaws, remember that Jesus desires authentic relationships far more than religious superstars. He wants to bring healing to your heart and give you an abundant life from the inside out.

Lord, thank you for working in my heart and preventing me from slipping into religious pretense. Help me be less concerned about my reputation than my relationship with you. Help me honestly acknowledge my failures so that I can receive forgiveness and healing. Guide me into a more genuine and authentic faith so that I can live the abundant life that you offer. In Jesus' name, Amen.

Personal Reflection

Consider your own reputation. Does your reputation reflect reality? Are you living for Christ or keeping up appearances? What might Christ say to you about the authenticity of your faith? Spend

Day 61

some time listening for his voice, and then end your quiet time today by thanking him for grace and loving guidance.

_____

_____

_____

_____

_____

_____

_____

_____

_____

_____

_____

_____

_____

_____

_____

Day 62
Wake Up!

Yesterday, we talked about the misconception that owls are wise. Although they have a reputation for being intelligent, they really aren't very smart. Owls make up for their subpar intelligence with other exceptional abilities though.

An owl's eyes, in particular, provide a distinct advantage over prey. The eyes of an owl can comprise up to 3% of its body weight, which doesn't seem like much until compared with human eyes, which are roughly 0.0003% of our body weight. Additionally, owl eyes are not round, but tubular, which enhances focusing ability and depth perception.

The nocturnal vision of owls also helps them thrive. Their eyes are particularly adaptable to different levels of light, enabling them to see well in both daylight and darkness. The superior night vision, combined with excellent hearing, gives owls the ability to locate and snatch unsuspecting prey in the dark.

The Christ followers in Sardis, which we also discussed yesterday, were behaving like unsuspecting prey. At one time, the church had followed Christ fervently and faithfully. Over time, however, their zeal began to wane, and their complacency metastasized until most members of the congregation "soiled their clothes with evil," (Revelation 3:4a). Their evil was like an owl gliding through the dark preparing to devour its prey. Jesus warned, "Wake up! Strengthen what little remains, for even what is left is almost dead," (Revelation 3:2a). They were completely unaware as their destruction crept nearer and nearer.

Complacency had clouded their vision and lulled them to sleep. The same can happen to you and me if we aren't careful. We must keep our eyes on Christ and stay alert. Owls aren't the smartest bird in the tree, but they make up for it with sharp vision and innate skill. If we keep our eyes on Jesus, he provides the resources, skills, and wisdom we need to fend off the enemy. We don't have to be the smartest, the best, or the strongest, we just need to stay focused on our Savior.

Lord, thank you for providing all the resources, skills, and wisdom I need to avoid the schemes of the enemy. Give me clear vision as I strive to follow you faithfully. Help me guard against complacency by diligently spending time in prayer, Bible study, fellowship, and service. Help me to set an example of diligence and faith. Strengthen me as I seek to protect myself and my faith community from attacks of the enemy. In Jesus' name, Amen.

Personal Reflection

Pray and ask God to show you if you've become complacent in any areas of your faith. Ask him to give you clear vision as you evaluate your spiritual alertness. Determine one step you can take in order to walk in greater vigilance today.

_____

_____

_____

_____

Day 63
Mole Hole

Smokey and Pepper love catching small creatures that trespass into our yard. On one occasion, they delivered a dead mole right to my back door. I wasn't aware we had any moles, but apparently there was at least one in the vicinity. Encountering the dead mole up close and personal stimulated my curiosity, so I did some reading up on moles and discovered one of the most bizarre behaviors ever.

You probably know that moles live underground. Their subterranean habitat keeps them warm and safe in winter, but the cold, hard ground also makes food hard to find. As a result, most moles prepare for the cold months by storing food in their burrows.

Here is where it starts to get weird. A mole's diet consists primarily of earthworms. Moles can't kill the worms before storing them or they'll decompose and rot. Therefore, a mole will injure or paralyze its worms to keep them alive but immobile. Each mole will store literally hundreds of worms to ensure that it has enough food for the winter.

The mole's behavior is disgusting from our perspective, but its strategy is keen. By choosing to store a resource that will not perish, the mole ensures its future flourishing. Although I'm not sure if I would consider a life of eating worms flourishing.

Jesus similarly instructs us to store up treasures that will not rot or rust. In Matthew 6, he teaches, "Don't store up treasures here on earth, where moths eat them and rust destroys them, and where thieves break in and steal. Store your treasures in heaven, where moths and rust cannot destroy, and thieves do not break in and steal," (Matthew 6:19–21). Earthly treasures will perish—your beauty will fade, your health will decline, and your body will die. Your possessions will end up at the dump and your money will be in someone else's bank account.

Fortunately, Jesus offers treasures that are far more valuable than temporary, external riches. Our Lord encourages us to store up heavenly treasures, which are lasting and life-giving. Heavenly treasures ensure flourishing both now, in the future, and for all eternity. We'll talk more about treasures tomorrow, but for now, let me just say that every earthly treasure will eventually be of no greater value than a molehill full of worms. Although the behavior of the mole is instinctive, you and I get to choose the type of treasures we will store. What are you going to choose today?

Lord, thank you for offering me treasures that have lasting value. Thank you for providing everything I need to flourish both now and in the future. Help me to invest my life in pursuits that will bear meaningful, lasting fruit in my life and in the lives of others. Teach me to view earthly treasures not as a goal but as a means of building imperishable riches. In Jesus' name, Amen.

Personal Reflection

Today, ask God to show you any areas of life in which you might be overly focused on earthly treasures. Do you devote more energy to improving appearance, status, position, possessions, or wealth than investing in God's Kingdom? Make a list of any perishable treasures that could be distracting you from building imperishable wealth. Ask God to show you how each earthly resource can instead be used as a means of storing up heavenly treasures.

Day 63

Day 64
Blood Buddies

If you are still reading these devotionals, you probably aren't squeamish. I should warn you, however, that today we'll be talking about vampire bats. Proceed at your own risk, although I highly recommend reading about these fascinating behaviors.

The primary cuisine of the vampire bat is, you guessed it, blood. They prefer to dine on large warm-blooded animals like horses and cows, but chickens will do in a pinch. The bats don't kill their food sources, so finding cooperative hosts can be difficult. Because the bats must eat at least every 48 hours to survive, they've developed a surprising survival strategy.

Believe it or not, vampire bats form complex social bonds akin to friendships. They first test out the relational waters with low-risk behaviors like grooming one another. Once low-level trust is established through grooming, one bat may decide to share a small amount of blood. If the second bat reciprocates, the new friends gradually build more trust by sharing increasing amounts of blood over time.

Vampire bats have mastered a behavior with which most humans struggle—sharing. As toddlers, we must learn to share, and even as adults we must resist the visceral urge to horde our resources. In 1 Timothy, Paul discusses the virtues of sharing.

> *Teach those who are rich in this world not to be proud*
> *and not to trust in their money, which is so unreliable.*
> *Their trust should be in God, who richly gives us all*

we need for our enjoyment. Tell them to use their money to do good. They should be rich in good works and generous to those in need, always being ready to share with others. By doing this they will be storing up their treasure as a good foundation for the future so that they may experience true life.

1 Timothy 6:17–19

Paul explains that giving away resources is critical to getting more. In fact, heavenly treasures and earthly treasures function inversely. If our goal is to amass worldly wealth, we'll lose everything. Yet, if we give everything we have, we'll gain eternal treasures.

Let's be clear that earthly treasures like money, positions, and titles aren't inherently harmful or evil. God blesses his people with abundant resources to do his work in the world. Our Father lavishly shares with us so that we can, in turn, share with the world.

Lord, thank you for richly blessing me with treasures that will never perish. I repent for behaving selfishly and prioritizing worthless things. Help me surrender every resource I have at my disposal to you. Give me greater faith in your ongoing provision and empower me to share generously with the world. Give me the wisdom to rightly prioritize my life so that I view material wealth and earthly status as a means of investing in your Kingdom and building heavenly treasures.

Personal Reflection

Prayerfully seek out opportunities to share today! You can share your skills by helping a co-worker complete a task. You can share monetary resources and bless someone with a financial need. You can share your time by calling someone who is lonely. You can share smiles, kind words, and encouragement. Best of all, you can share the Gospel message!

Day 65

Storing up Treasures in ... the Dirt?

One morning when I was around 5 years old, I gathered my most treasured knick-knacks and placed them in a small tin box. The contents of the box represented a random assortment of little girl items. I don't remember precisely, but I believe I included a couple of heart-shaped magnets, some small pieces of colorful paper, miniature-colored pens, and several pieces of gaudy costume jewelry. Because I wanted to keep my treasures safe, I buried the box under my favorite tree. From time to time I would unbury it, look at all my treasures, then rebury the box.

My stash of treasures brought delight to my heart, but it illustrates an ugly reality. You and I are born selfish. Instead of sharing my treasures with others, I hid them. My treasure stash made me happy, but in hoarding treasures, I deprived myself of a greater joy. I totally missed the opportunity to share my toys with friends, play dress up with the jewelry, and color together on the paper. Yet, due to my selfishness, my favorite things sat unused in a box under the dirt.

When we hoard our treasures, we waste them and deprive ourselves of more valuable blessings. Storing up earthly treasures even drains vital resources and inhibits future flourishing. In Luke 12, Jesus shares a parable about the futility of hoarding perishable resources.

> *Then [Jesus] told them a story: "A rich man had a fertile farm that produced fine crops. He said to himself,*

'What should I do? I don't have room for all my crops.' Then he said, 'I know! I'll tear down my barns and build bigger ones. Then I'll have room enough to store all my wheat and other goods. And I'll sit back and say to myself, "My friend, you have enough stored away for years to come. Now take it easy! Eat, drink, and be merry!"' "But God said to him, 'You fool! You will die this very night. Then who will get everything you worked for?'

The rich man didn't bury his treasure; he hoarded it in a big barn. Instead of feeding the poor or feasting with friends, he kept everything for himself. He could have shared the blessings of God, invested in the lives of others, and gained treasures beyond measure, but instead, the rich man lost everything.

Like the rich man, I lost my treasure, too. I have no memory of where the little box ended up. My cheap treasures could still be buried for all I know. Similarly, Jesus doesn't tell us what happened to the rich man's wealth—because it doesn't matter. Temporary treasures simply don't bring lasting fulfillment and flourishing.

Jesus wants us to understand that unlike earthly treasures, our heavenly treasures last forever. The reason they are eternal is that at the most basic level, they represent people. Our treasures are friends and family with whom we'll spend eternity. Our treasures are individuals who accepted Christ because we shared our time, talents, and resources.

Lord, thank you for providing me with an abundance of resources so that I can bless others. Help me bear your image well by generously sharing with people around me. Show me how I can steward my time, talents, and resources more effectively in order to make a greater Kingdom impact. Please reveal whether I am hoarding any treasures for myself, either intentionally or unknowingly. I pray that you would provide financial increase in my life so that I can give more away. In Jesus' name, Amen.

Personal Reflection

Consider the three primary types of resources available to you: time, wealth, and talents. For each category, think about how you "spend" your resources, and ask yourself the following questions.

> Do you prioritize sharing your resources or do you first store up what you think you might need for yourself?
>
> Does your resource management indicate that you have more faith in God's provision or in the resources themselves?
>
> Are you neglecting to utilize any of the resources that might be available to you out of oversight, fear, or selfishness?
>
> What is one step you can take to steward one resource more wisely, generously, and faithfully?

_____

_____

_____

_____

_____

_____

Day 66
Fall Fragrances

Fall isn't my favorite time of the year, but I do love the smells of the season. I enjoy some scents simply because they smell good to me. For instance, I fill my house with pumpkin spice candles, and I drench myself in clove, cardamom, and cinnamon essential oils. Other scents are pleasing because they evoke powerful associations. When I smell a pumpkin pie, I think of happy times and shared holiday meals with family. When I smell a campfire, I think of roasting marshmallows with my boys and cuddling with my husband. The scents fill me with joy because they represent meaningful parts of my life.

Did you know that God has favorite smells too? Throughout Scripture, God says that the offerings of his people are a "pleasing aroma" (Exodus 29:19). In the Old Testament, the pleasing scents arose from animal sacrifices burning on the altar. It probably smelled a lot like a backyard barbeque! Even though we no longer sacrifice animals, our offerings still smell wonderful to God. Instead of goats, cows, and birds, we offer ourselves as living sacrifices (Romans 12:1). When we surrender our plans, purposes, gifts, and resources, God delights in our offerings, and we smell delightful to him.

Offerings smell pleasant to God because they represent meaningful truths. The sacrifices of ancient Israel were declarations of their obedience, faith, and devotion to God. On a deeper level their sacrifices foreshadowed the coming death and atoning work of Jesus.

When you and I offer ourselves, we please God because we smell like Jesus. Paul instructs, "Therefore be imitators of God, as beloved children; and walk in love, just as Christ also loved you and gave Himself up for us, an offering and a sacrifice to God as a fragrant aroma," (Ephesians 5:1–2). When we sacrifice our desires, wants, and resources for the cause of Christ, we smell like God's Son. Further, our offerings please God because they spread the scent of Jesus throughout the world. Paul celebrates that God "uses us to spread the knowledge of Christ everywhere, like a sweet perfume," (2 Corinthians 2:14b).

Sacrifice isn't easy, but it's worthwhile. Our world is filled with the stench of death, but you and I have the opportunity to exude the sweet scent of life in Christ. When we show love and share the Gospel, we smell even better than pumpkin spice!

Lord, thank you for offering your Son, Jesus, as a fragrant sacrifice for my sins. Help me to spread the scent of my Savior through sharing his love. Forgive me for too often smelling like the world instead of smelling like Jesus. Help me surrender my resources, gifts, time, and plans to you. Help me surrender my pride and fear as I boldly seek opportunities to share the Gospel. I pray that my life would be a fragrant aroma to you. In Jesus' name, Amen.

Personal Reflection

What can you offer as a pleasing aroma to God today? Make a point of showing love and/or sharing the Gospel today, even if it takes an extra effort.

_____

_____

Day 66

Day 67
Sour Smells

If I had a superpower, it would be my sense of smell. I routinely smell things that no one else can detect. At one point when the kids were in elementary school, my car developed a sour odor. No one else could detect the scent or find the source of my complaint. Wesley, Asher, and Abel thought I was going crazy.

Finally, I couldn't stand the smell any longer and I decided to give the car a thorough cleaning. I felt great validation and vindication when I found the offending odor. Tucked away in the pocket behind one of the seats was a closed container of milk. A closed container of SOUR milk. I had smelled the bad milk through the material of the seat and through the closed plastic container. No one has doubted my acute sense of smell since that day.

Yesterday, we talked about aromas that God finds pleasing, but God also finds certain scents repellant. While our love and self-sacrifice smell delightful to God, our sin and disobedience stink. When we disrespect God's standards, abuse his grace, and dishonor his family, we smell foul. Even worse, God says that if you disobey me and "act with hostility against Me . . . I will not smell your soothing aromas," (Leviticus 26:27, 31). This passage makes me think about a garbage dumpster on a hot summer day. The odor of hot sewage makes it impossible to enjoy any pleasant smells like fresh grass and fragrant flowers. In a similar manner, our stinky sin overpowers the pleasing scent of our sacrifice.

Transgressions stink because all sin is ultimately rooted in death. Psalm 38 helps us understand this concept. The Psalmist writes, "My wounds fester and stink because of my foolish sins," (Psalm 38:5). Bodily wounds, if not treated quickly and thoroughly, can fester, become infected, and even cause death. The worsening illness is accompanied by an odor that increases steadily and culminates with the stench of death. Similarly, our sin often incurs physical, emotional, mental, or relational wounds. We probably won't fester and stink in a literal manner, but the odor of our infection will overpower the aroma of Christ in our lives.

Fortunately, our Heavenly Father loves us even when we are stinky. Even if your sin is well-hidden and stinks only a little, God can still smell it. Like the rotten milk tucked away in my car, he wants to help you find the sin and get rid of it. You may have to do a little digging to find the source of the stink, but God is right there with you guiding your search.

Lord, thank you for providing a life of growth and health rather than bondage to death. Help me identify the stinky sins in my own life so that I can repent and receive healing. I confess that I have knowingly sinned against you in the past and I ask forgiveness. I pray that I would see my transgressions through your eyes and be as repulsed by them as you are. Prompt me to seek your guidance daily and live in obedience. Thank you for loving me even when I don't deserve it. In Jesus' name, Amen.

Personal Reflection

Pray and ask God to show you any stinky sins in your life, big or small. Ask him to reveal which issues need immediate attention. Write down two or three opportunities for growth. For each item, identify one strategy for replacing the stinky smell with a pleasant aroma.

Day 68
Yummy in the Tummy

By now, you're probably approaching the holiday season. I love everything about the holidays: decorating, family time, giving gifts, and special church services. I also love holiday food. The buttery, sugary holiday fare brings joy to my soul. Unfortunately, rich food does not bring joy to my stomach. A couple of hours after I indulge in a rich meal, indigestion and nausea begin to creep in. The food that I initially enjoyed turns into stomach acid and regret. Perhaps one day I will learn to pass on the heavier dishes, but probably not.

Just as we consume food with our mouth, we also consume the world around us with our eyes and ears. We are inundated with content—movies, shows, podcasts, music, social media, books, and more! Unless we're discerning, what we consume can make us sick in heart and soul. According to Paul, indulging our appetite for "earthly things" leads to destruction (Philippians 3:18–19).

While numerous passages in Scripture describe such "earthly things", there is no single, comprehensive list. God knows that rote rule following leads to legalism, rather than a deeper communion with him. Recall the Pharisees, who compulsively followed the Law and whom Jesus called "whitewashed tombs" (Matthew 23:27). Although the Pharisees consumed an astounding magnitude of Scripture, they were deathly ill on the inside.

Rather than creating legalistic, and often arbitrary, lists of what we can and can't consume, we should simply fix our eyes on things that honor God. Paul instructs Christ followers to "Fix your thoughts on what is true, and honorable, and right, and pure, and lovely, and admirable. Think about things that are excellent and worthy of praise," (Phil 4:8 NLT). Instead of junk food for the soul, Paul exhorts us to consume nourishment that will equip us to thrive.

I'm already looking forward to the delicious cucumbers, tomatoes, and peppers from my garden next summer. They not only taste good, but they are good for my body. When we consume nourishment that is healthy, our bodies become healthier. When we consume unhealthy food, our bodies become weaker. Our spiritual health functions in a similar way. Before you consume media, prayerfully determine whether your choice will bring health or harm. Let's choose to dine wisely.

Lord, thank you for the avenues of media that enable me to learn more about you and grow in my faith. Give me the wisdom to discern between content that brings life and content that brings destruction. Give me the self-discipline to turn away from any content that dishonors you. Help me take breaks from the constant stream of media to enjoy this beautiful world in which I live. Teach me to mindfully enjoy creation and allow it to nourish my soul. Guide my thoughts toward that which is true, honorable, right, pure, lovely, admirable, excellent, and worthy of praise. In Jesus' name, Amen.

Personal Reflection

Spend a few moments meditating on your mental and spiritual "diet." Identify some of the junky content you are consuming and search for ways you can replace it with healthier options. You can take a technology time-out and go outside. You can replace unhealthy content with faith-based media. I suggest checking out www.TheBibleProject.com.

Their videos are excellent for any age group and their podcasts will take your understanding of Scripture to the next level. The Bible Project content is a Robinson family favorite!

_____

_____

_____

_____

_____

_____

_____

_____

_____

_____

_____

_____

_____

_____

_____

_____

Day 69
Milking It

The forerunner of Smokey and Pepper was a mini schnauzer named Schmutzie. She was a gift for my 20th birthday and my favorite present ever. Let me tell you a little about her arrival.

I desperately wanted a puppy for my birthday, and I knew I wanted a schnauzer. My parents love dogs as much as I do, so they were happy to oblige. As my birthday approached, they helped me find a litter of mini-schnauzers in a neighboring state. We talked to the owner over the phone and confirmed our intention to adopt the sole female pup. We then made arrangements to pick her up as soon as she was weaned, eating solid food, and ready for her new home.

When the pick-up day arrived, weather conditions were abominable, but I simply couldn't wait another day. We drove through freezing weather, sleeting rain, and icy roads to get my girl. I still remember seeing her for the first time and falling fiercely in love with her. She was small, soft, and a little sassy. I knew she was perfect for me.

When we arrived back at home, I fed Schmutzie her dinner and immediately realized we had a problem. Despite what her previous owner had said, my pup had no idea how to eat solid food. Undeterred, I considered the situation a bonding opportunity. Nothing could diminish my joy over adopting my little Schmutzie. So, for the next two days I fed Schmutzie milk from a medicine dropper every two hours, morning and night. As the days passed, I transitioned her to a paste of mashed dog food and milk, then soggy dog food, and finally dry dog food in her own bowl. I was so proud—I felt like my baby had graduated from college.

God, likewise, loves to help his children grow and mature. When we are spiritual infants, we don't know how to nourish ourselves, so our patient Father provides extra care. Just as I had fed Schmutzie from the medicine dropper, our Father feeds us pure spiritual milk in the form of easily digestible truths and basic tenants of faith. As we grow in maturity, he begins to feed us heartier, richer meals, helping us understand the complexities of his character and our responsibilities as part of his Kingdom.

At every point in the process of growth, we must take initiative to receive nourishment from the Lord. According to 1 Peter 2:2, "Like newborn babies, you must crave pure spiritual milk so that you will grow into a full experience of salvation." Even as infants in our faith, we can become stagnant if we don't pursue godly growth. But God desires that we grow into mature faith.

Like a good Father, God offers ample opportunities for you and I to grow. He has provided the wisdom of Scripture, the gift of the Holy Spirit, the protection of community, and so much more! God equips you with every resource that you need to experience the fullness of his salvation.

Lord, thank you for giving me opportunities to grow in skills, knowledge, and maturity. Open my eyes to every opportunity, and motivate me to take advantage of each. Give me a hunger and a thirst for your Word and your presence. Help me be intentional about making growth a consistent part of my life. Show me the specific areas in which you would have me grow in this season of my life. I praise you for patiently leading me to the right growth opportunities in every season. In Jesus' name, Amen.

Personal Reflection

Seek God's will regarding his plan for your spiritual growth. Prayerfully self-reflect about how you can grow in each of the following areas: prayer, Bible study, community, self-discipline, and integrity. Allow God to show you any other areas of growth he desires to see in your life. Write down your thoughts and impressions. We'll further reflect on these growth opportunities tomorrow.

_____

_____

_____

_____

_____

_____

_____

_____

_____

_____

_____

_____

Day 70
Num-Nums

Yesterday we talked about God's will for continuous spiritual growth in our lives. As a caring Father, our Lord guides us to maturity through avenues befitting each stage of our spiritual development. Unfortunately, we don't always take advantage of the opportunities he provides. We must partner with God and take the initiative to grow. Let me illustrate with a personal example.

When my son, Abel, was a toddler, he loved to be fed "bite-bites" and "num-nums," which were basically any food. I was happy to oblige because hand feeding him worked to my advantage. Abel was messier than the average kid by orders of magnitude, if you can wrap your head around that. Feeding him was one way I could contain the debris field he created during meals.

Abel and I continued our symbiotic mealtime behavior on and off until he was well into kindergarten. During one particular steak dinner when Abel asked me to cut up his steak and feed him "bite-bites," Wesley put his foot down. My husband forbade me to feed Abel by hand anymore. He knew that the mealtime food mess was far less of a problem than Abel's lack of self-feeding skills. Because I had fed him for so long, he could barely use a spoon or fork. Instead of awkwardly using the utensils, Abel would simply eat with his hands whenever he could get away with it. Because Abel had no desire to use utensils, it took years for him to eat properly with a spoon, knife, and fork.

In a similar manner, many Christ followers are content to be spoon-fed the Word of God and remain spiritual infants. In Hebrews 5, God's people face reprimand for failing to grow up.

You have been believers so long now that you ought to be teaching others. Instead, you need someone to teach you again the basic things about God's word. You are like babies who need milk and cannot eat solid food. For someone who lives on milk is still an infant and doesn't know how to do what is right. Solid food is for those who are mature, who through training have the skill to recognize the difference between right and wrong.

Hebrews 5:12–14

Instead of growing to maturity and learning about God for themselves, these Christ followers were being complacent and lazy. They were content to subsist on baby food and be spoon fed by someone else. Because they never took the initiative to grow in maturity, they couldn't tell the difference between healthy nourishment and poisoned food.

When we neglect to grow, we remain in a vulnerable state. We aren't mature enough to nourish ourselves or strong enough to defend ourselves. We can't discern the truth because we've failed to learn the truth for ourselves. Because we rely on regurgitated information, we never strengthen the muscles needed to guard against deception and attack. By the time we should be mature enough to teach others, we haven't even developed the skills that we need to safely navigate the world. Our problem is not lack of resources, it's lack of motivation. Let's stop being content with "num-nums" and start digging into the meat of God's Word!

Lord, thank you for providing nutrition fitting each season of my spiritual growth. Give me a desire to grow into the fullness of your plan for me. Give me a hunger for the meat of your Word so that I can better discern right from wrong. Grow my self-discipline so that I am faithful to spend time in prayer and Bible study every day. I ask you to show me the specific areas in which you want me to grow in this season of my life. In Jesus' name, Amen.

Personal Reflection

Review the growth opportunities you wrote down yesterday. Prayerfully review your list and ask God if anything needs to be added, removed, or revised. Then, use your list to make a personal growth plan. As you craft your plan, list each growth opportunity along with *why* you need to grow in each area, *how* you plan to grow, and *when* you will work on each skill. Set measurable short-term and long-term goals for each item. Finally, identify any obstacles and write down a few strategies for reframing each obstacle into an opportunity or removing it from your path.

_____

_____

_____

_____

_____

_____

_____

Day 71
Troublesome Tornadoes

In Alabama, tornadoes can occur any month of the year, but November is one of the highest probability months. The warm air of fall moves out as the cold air of winter moves in, creating perfect conditions for a tornado. The clash of warm and cold air creates atmospheric instability and ultimately the funnel clouds that create so much destruction.

Like the warm and cold air, the principle of opposing forces is found throughout nature—light and dark, wet and dry, acid and base, positive and negative. These polar opposites simply can't coexist. If forced together, the opposing elements either create instability or undergo fundamental change.

A similar principle applies in our spiritual life. Paul explains,

> *Don't team up with those who are unbelievers. How can righteousness be a partner with wickedness? How can light live with darkness? What harmony can there be between Christ and the devil? How can a believer be a partner with an unbeliever?*

2 Corinthians 6:14–15

Two opposing entities can't coexist. If we are Christ followers, we can't live like unbelievers. If we try to force the two opposing belief systems together, our minds will be filled with instability and turmoil. Our thoughts and motivations will swirl like a funnel cloud, causing

235

destruction and strife. The victims of this storm are inner peace, confident faith, relational unity, and personal integrity.

Instead, our lives should reflect our partnership with Christ. Because we are united with him, we should reflect his character. Instead of an inner storm, unity with the Prince of Peace brings peace to every area of our life.

Lord, thank you for inner peace, confident faith, and relational unity. Help me reflect your character and live with integrity. Reveal any behaviors, patterns of speech, or relationships that are not aligned with your light and love. Give me the courage and strength to make changes that will better align my life with your lordship. In Jesus' name, Amen.

Personal Reflection

Spend some extra time in prayer today. Ask God to reveal any behaviors, patterns of speech, or relationships that are inconsistent with his lordship. Ask him to show you one positive change you can make today.

_____

_____

_____

_____

_____

_____

_____

Day 72
The Sound of a Storm

I have heard that tornadoes sound like a freight train or a jet engine. The roar is not only caused by rapidly moving air, but also by the debris thrashed by the vortex. I have never experienced such a severe storm in person, and I hope to keep it that way. The Prophet Elijah, however, weathered a massive storm firsthand.

Go out and stand before me on the mountain," the Lord told him. And as Elijah stood there, the Lord passed by, and a mighty windstorm hit the mountain. It was such a terrible blast that the rocks were torn loose, but the Lord was not in the wind. After the wind there was an earthquake, but the Lord was not in the earthquake. And after the earthquake there was a fire, but the Lord was not in the fire. And after the fire there was the sound of a gentle whisper.

1 Kings 19:11–12

The way God typically communicates with his people isn't loud and flashy, like a storm. Our Father speaks in a gentle whisper.

I think we would all agree that we want to hear God's voice. We want direction for our lives, we want guidance for our decisions, we want clarity for our relationships. Although we are eager to hear his voice, we rarely quiet our lives enough to hear him. We are inundated by a constant storm of sounds and images. We are so accustomed to the mental and literal noise, that when a rare moment of quietude arises, we grab our phones and start scrolling. God may be prepared to speak with you, but the volume of your life is too loud to hear his whisper. Your patient Father is waiting for you to turn down the volume.

Lord, thank you for speaking softly and gently to my heart as a loving Father. Help me be purposeful about quieting the tenor of my life. Help me be intentional about finding moments each day to listen for your gentle whisper. I repent of asking for guidance without listening for your response. Guide me and empower me as I cultivate more robust times of fellowship with you. In Jesus' name, Amen.

Personal Reflection

Survey your surroundings right now. Is your devotional time quiet and distraction free? Are you giving yourself time to listen for the gentle whisper of your Father as you read and pray? Take at least one step toward creating an environment more conducive to fellowship with God in your daily devotional time or in moments throughout your day.

_____

_____

_____

_____

_____

_____

Day 72

Day 73
Happy Birthday to Me!

Since we are approaching Thanksgiving, I want to spend a few days thinking about gratitude. Since we are approaching my birthday, I'd like to share a bit about my birth. First, let's read Psalm 139:13–14.

For you created my inmost being;
you knit me together in my mother's womb.
I praise you because I am fearfully and wonderfully made;
your works are wonderful,
I know that full well.

Before I was born, my parents had been married for several years, and they were hoping to have a baby soon. Tragically though, their home caught fire, and my father passed away at the age of 25. Unbeknownst to him, my mother already suspected that she was several weeks pregnant.

Despite the enemy's horrible plan for our family, God protected my mother, and God protected me inside her womb. So, with her husband gone and her home destroyed, my mother moved in with her parents, my Gram and Pops. We lived with them for a few years as she began rebuilding her life. I became so close to my grandparents that my first word was even "Pops."

I want you to see that throughout our tragedy, God not only protected and provided for us, but he set us on a path toward a good future. I'm not saying we didn't face any more trials, but God brought us through those as well. As Jeremiah 29:11 says, God's plans for us are prosperity, not destruction.

Despite the devastating circumstances under which my life began, I have so much to be thankful for—a mother who provided an example of strength and resilience, my Gram and Pops who loved us dearly and provided a place for us to heal and grow, a step-father who has become the best dad and granddad ever, and a Heavenly Father who not only protected me in a real, literal way, but has also blessed me in more ways than I can count. I can praise him because I am fearfully and wonderfully made, and I know that his works are wonderful.

Lord, thank you for watching over me in every circumstance. I trust that you can bring good from even the most difficult trial. Help me keep my focus on you and the blessings you provide daily. Guide me as I seek to walk in the good plan you have for my life. In Jesus' name, Amen.

Personal Reflection

Meditate on trials that you have experienced. Look for ways in which God has protected you or blessed you in the midst of your struggles.

Take some time to express gratitude to your heavenly Father.

_____

_____

_____

_____

_____

_____

Day 74
Happy Birthday to Asher!

Yesterday, I shared a personal story about my own birth. Today, I would like to share a story about the birth of my first child, Asher. The circumstances surrounding his birth were not tragic like my own, but Asher's conception was a shocking and life-changing development. Although Wesley and I were surprised, God wasn't. I'm so thankful that the Lord ordained Asher's life, even though he wasn't part of my own plan.

As a young woman, I had my plans for my life all laid out. Wesley and I got married, I finished my bachelor's degree, and I began a master's degree program in biblical studies. I planned to complete that degree and proceed immediately into a PhD program. I would complete that degree and then begin teaching seminary classes. That was my plan, and it didn't include having children.

Soon after I began the master's program, I started having strange health issues. Yet, I was extremely active at that time, and I assumed my physical symptoms were due to over-exercise. As a result, I ignored the symptoms and continued on with life as usual. Weeks turned into months with the same physical issues, yet I continued to ignore them. My mom suggested that I might be pregnant, but I laughed. Finally, my mother and aunt conspired to force me to take action. They went to the drug store, bought a pregnancy test, brought it to my house, and asked me to take it. I complied, knowing that the result would be negative.

You may have guessed by now that the results were not negative, and I was not happy. I literally collapsed to the bathroom floor, weeping. My sweet Wesley, who was as shocked as me, remained calm, gathered me from the floor, and gently told my mom and my aunt that they should probably leave until I calmed down.

A couple of days later, my mom accompanied me to the doctor for an ultrasound, where we discovered that I was 16 weeks, that's 4 months, pregnant! Little Asher was waving his arms and legs like he was saying hello. At that moment, I began to fall in love.

Throughout the pregnancy, I continued to struggle with the massive shift in the trajectory of my life. But when Asher was born, I was certain that he was the biggest blessing I had ever received. We even named him Asher, which means blessed and happy!

Even though I hadn't planned for a baby or desired one, even though I was mad at God, even though I felt like my life had been derailed, God was STILL blessing me. I'm so glad God's knowledge is bigger, and his plans are better than my own.

When I think about Asher's conception, I think of David's words in Psalm 139:15–16.

> *My frame was not hidden from you*
> *when I was made in the secret place,*
> *when I was woven together in the depths of the earth.*
> *Your eyes saw my unformed body;*
> *all the days ordained for me were written in your book*
> *before one of them came to be.*

Psalm 139:15–16

You and I exist within one finite moment in time and space, but God sees everything, everywhere, for all time. Our perspective on life is limited, but our limitless God sees and knows everything. Therefore, he knows what is best for us, even when we don't. He knew me in my mother's womb, and he knew my boys in my womb. Even better, his plans for each of us are wonderful. My prayer is that we would all learn to trust him more. Even when life doesn't go as planned or expected, God is still working in our lives in a powerful way.

Lord, I believe that you have good plans for my life. Thank you for remaining faithful even when I doubt you. Help me to trust you more and have faith in your goodness. Give me the wisdom and strength to walk in obedience, even when your plans don't align with what I expect. Help me to view disappointments as opportunities to draw closer to you. In Jesus' name, Amen

Personal Reflection

Meditate on any unexpected twists in your own life and evaluate your response. Did you react in faith or fear? Did you trust God or doubt his goodness? Consider how you might respond with greater trust and faith in the future.

_____

_____

_____

_____

_____

_____

_____

_____

Day 75
Thankful for Earthworms

The last couple of days, we talked about having gratitude throughout the twists and turns of life. Twists, turns, and trials are somewhat like earthworms. I have trouble being thankful for earthworms. They are slimy and brown. When it rains, they crawl onto my patio, then dry up and stick like glue when the rain dries. However, unlike army worms, earthworms are beneficial for my garden. As they burrow through the dirt, they aerate the soil, which helps water and nutrients penetrate to the roots of plants. Additionally, they eat bacteria and microscopic pests, then excrete nourishing minerals. I'm always happy to see an earthworm as long as it stays in the garden. To say it another way, I like the benefits of earthworms, just not the earthworms themselves.

Similarly, I don't like trials, but they can promote growth. James explains:

> *Dear brothers and sisters, when troubles of any kind come your way, consider it an opportunity for great joy. For you know that when your faith is tested, your endurance has a chance to grow. So let it grow, for when your endurance is fully developed, you will be perfect and complete, needing nothing.*
>
> ### *James 1:2–4*

Just as the earthworm burrows through the dirt, deposits nutrients, and loosens hardened soil, our trials deposit endurance and character in our soul. They soften the hardened places in our hearts and create opportunities for growth.

Now, forgive me if I strain the metaphor, but the worm must navigate his dark, hard path or disaster can strike. When he emerges above the soil he can be cooked by the sun or eaten by a bird. Likewise, when we try to create our own solutions or find our way out of trials without God, we not only forsake the benefits of perseverance, but can reap destructive consequences. Let's stay the course and thank God for the opportunity to grow.

Jesus, thank you for using every trial to make me stronger. Help me to seek solutions in your Word rather than seeking my own way out. Allow me to see my trials through your eyes and take joy in the rewards that I will reap. I repent of doubting you in the past. Guide me to new levels of endurance and faith. Help me to follow your example of faithful service in the midst of my struggle. In Jesus' name, Amen.

Personal Reflection

Meditate on any "earthworms" in your past. How has God helped you grow through past struggles? What can you learn that will help you more successfully navigate trials in the future?

_____

_____

_____

_____

_____

Day 76
Thankful for Peace

When I think about places that make me feel peaceful, I think of the beach, and I am definitely thankful for the beach. Now, this devotional might be more appropriate for the summer, but it's nice to dream of the beach when it's cold outside, right?

I love everything about the beach. I love the sound of the waves and the feel of the breeze. I love the sun on my skin and the sand under my feet. I love floating in the water and swimming in the surf. I love snorkeling in the shallows and fishing in the deeps.

But enough summertime dreaming. If we evaluate the beach analytically, it is less than peaceful and actually quite dangerous. The wind can be turbulent, and the waves are loud. The undertow can pull you out to sea, and the water can drown you. The sand can chafe, and the sun can burn. Sharks can bite and jellyfish can sting. You get the point. So why do we feel peaceful at the beach? I don't have an answer to that, but the beach does provide an apt analogy for life.

Life can be hard and frustrating. People will hurt you and offend you. You will weep, grieve, and mourn. Remember that even Jesus tells us, "In this world you will have trouble" (John 16:33). Yet, Jesus also says, "Peace I leave with you; my peace I give you. I do not give to you as the world gives. Do not let your hearts be troubled and do not be afraid" (John 14:27). We want to have the peace that Jesus talks about, but how can we possibly have peace in a world full of strife? Perhaps we need a deeper understanding of peace.

Secular culture would describe peace as the absence of illness, abundant financial resources, a lucrative career, and the absence of conflict. Jesus offers a different perspective. Our Savior promises peace in the midst of troubles. He explains, "I have told you these things, so that in me you may have peace. In this world you will have trouble. But take heart! I have overcome the world," (John 16:33). When Jesus says "I have told you these things" he was talking about his own death and the dispersion of his disciples. That certainly doesn't sound peaceful.

Jesus is teaching us how to have a correct view of peace. Peace doesn't mean that problems go away, that we will always be healthy, and that we will have lots of money. Think of the beach. At the beach, we feel peaceful despite the noise, wind, heat, and dangerous creatures. So, peace doesn't come from perfect circumstances. Perfect circumstances will never happen. Our peace comes from knowing that Jesus will never abandon us. He is protecting us in the midst of our trials, and nothing can separate us from his love.

Lord, thank you for protecting me through every trial and providing peace that isn't based on circumstances. Give me the perseverance to lean into you rather than pulling away when I am struggling. Help me to base my trust on your Word rather than my emotions. I pray that my peace of mind and heart would encourage others and cause them to seek you. In Jesus' name, Amen.

Personal Reflection

Meditate on situations that bring you peace and situations that disrupt your peace. Do you feel peaceful only in the absence of hardship or is your peace rooted in your faith in Christ? As you go through your day today, be mindful of your thoughts and emotions. Take captive any anxious thoughts and remind yourself that the peace of Christ is available to you.

Day 76

Day 77
Thankful for Rest

I recently learned an interesting fact about the ocean that likely contributes to the peaceful feelings we have at the beach. Ocean waves have the frequency of twelve cycles per minute which is the average breathing frequency of a sleeping human. The waves help our bodies subconsciously attune to rhythms of rest.

We've already talked about the importance of rest in a previous devo, but I want to revisit the topic today. Rest is an integral part of our mind, body, and soul. We were literally created to enjoy God's rest. When God finished crafting the universe, he rested and invited creation to rest with him. According to Hebrews, "[God's] rest has been ready since he made the world," (Hebrews 4:3b). Further, "God's rest is there for people to enter, but those who first heard this good news failed to enter because they disobeyed God," (Hebrews 4:6). First Adam and Eve and then the people of Israel chose to go their own way instead of entering God's rest.

Fortunately, our gracious Father hasn't rescinded his offer of rest. Since God's past followers failed to experience his rest, "God set another time for entering his rest, and that time is today," (Hebrews 4:7). You and I have access to the rest of God right here and now!

But what, exactly, is God's rest? Rest isn't necessarily napping on the beach, although that might be one component. True rest is a deep and abiding peace that comes from the salvation of Christ. We can experience relief from fear, anxiety, rejection, unforgiveness, anger, and insecurity through the love of our savior. True rest is also rooted in faith and hope. Because we trust our Savior, we look forward to a more complete rest for all of creation. We eagerly anticipate the end of death and the beginning of an eternity with our loved ones.

The theology of rest should impact your life in tangible ways. You can enjoy rhythms of rest and naps on the beach because you trust in God's provision. You can overcome insecurity because your identity is rooted in Christ. You can release fear, unforgiveness, anger, and rejection because Christ's perfect love abides in your heart. I could go on and on, but let's simply close with the words of Jesus.

> *Then Jesus said, "Come to me, all of you who are weary and carry heavy burdens, and I will give you rest. Take my yoke upon you. Let me teach you, because I am humble and gentle at heart, and you will find rest for your souls. For my yoke is easy to bear, and the burden I give you is light."*
>
> **Matthew 11:28–30**

Lord, thank you for making a way for me to enter into your rest. I repent of worry, fear, insecurity, unforgiveness, and anger. Help me release my struggles to you, trust in your provision, and rest in your love. Guide me as I seek to implement and maintain healthy patterns of rest in my life. I pray that my heart would be so full of peace that no external circumstance would be able to disrupt my rest in you. In Jesus' name, Amen.

Personal Reflection

In a previous devotional, we talked about healthy rhythms of sleep and physical rest. Reassess those habits and ask God if you need further growth. Also ask God to reveal whether you might need mental or emotional rest in the form of release from harmful thoughts,

mindsets, or emotions. Make time this week to find a restful space
and continue praying about your patterns of rest.

_____

_____

_____

_____

_____

_____

_____

_____

_____

_____

_____

_____

_____

_____

Day 78
Thankful for Family

Parenting skills in the animal kingdom vary wildly. For instance, emperor penguins are exceptional dads. After the female lays her eggs, she abandons the family for a two-month vacation at sea. The male stays behind to warm the eggs with his body for the duration. Since he can't leave the eggs unsheltered in the cold Antarctic temperatures, he has to endure the entire period of time without food. On the opposite extreme, panda bears are notorious for their parenting behavior. Female pandas often bear twins but will only care for the stronger of the two while ignoring the weaker. Even worse, grizzly bears will eat their offspring if food is scarce.

Family can be a complex and sensitive topic. The intimacy of family bonds fosters vulnerability and strong emotions. Our interactions with family can evoke both the fiercest love and the deepest animosity. Wounds from a family member often hurt the most and take the longest to heal because they create harm within a context that is supposed to be safe.

You may feel like your family is the most dysfunctional group of people on the planet. In reality, though, no one has a perfect family. Perfect families don't exist because perfect people don't exist. As we navigate life, the people in our family see our greatest strengths and our deepest flaws. Together, we experience joyful victories, devastating trials, and embarrassing mistakes. Most likely, your family isn't more dysfunctional than the average, you simply aren't aware of the dysfunction happening behind everyone else's closed doors.

Through family, we receive training for life. In the context of family, we experience love, grace, and joy, but we also experience resentment, conflict, and disappointment. We might even experience betrayal, rejection, or abuse. Our response to such trauma or frustration is typically influenced by behavior we've seen modeled within the family. However, we have the capacity to choose how we will respond to each situation.

In fact, our response to family can serve as a barometer for our quality of our life. We can choose the path of bitterness and unforgiveness, blaming every personal failure on bad parenting and inadequate love. Alternately, we can take proactive measures to become relationally and emotionally healthy so that we don't perpetuate the same behaviors that were hurtful to us. Just as important, we can choose to forgive faults, grow in patience, grow in grace, and grow in God's love. According to 1 Peter 4:8, "Most important of all, continue to show deep love for each other, for love covers a multitude of sins."

Responding to family trauma with love, grace, and forgiveness doesn't mean that we allow dysfunction to have an ongoing impact on our life. We might need to set healthy boundaries with family, limit contact, or in extreme cases, cease contact completely. Prayer and professional counseling are excellent tools to help you heal, set healthy boundaries, and develop thriving relationships in every area of life.

Lord, thank you for using my family to help me grow in patience, kindness, and love. Help me to work on my own weaknesses and faults instead of pointing out the flaws in others. Help me see the best in others rather than the worst. Give me the grace to forgive even the ugliest offenses so that I can walk in joy, freedom, and obedience. Show me what I can learn from the mistakes of those who have hurt me as well as from the wounds I've inflicted on others. Guide me as I seek to grow in love, serve my family, and set healthy boundaries. In Jesus' name, Amen.

Personal Reflection

Ask God to search your heart and reveal whether you are harboring unforgiveness against any family members. Repent of your unforgiveness, surrender the offense to God, and ask Him to heal your wounds. Also ask God to reveal whether you need to ask forgiveness for any hurt or offense you caused. Consider speaking to a spiritual mentor or professional counselor to guide you.

_____

_____

_____

_____

_____

_____

_____

_____

_____

_____

_____

Day 79
Thankful for Patience

Orchids are among the most unique and beautiful species of flower on the planet. The orchid family is so large and diverse that a quick overview is virtually impossible. The most common type of orchid, however, is the phalaenopsis. This colorful variety is native to Asia and Australia, but it can be purchased in most grocery stores near you.

Grocery store orchids are a point of endless temptation and frustration for me. The beautiful flowers beckon me and beg me to take them home. Yet, I know that as soon as the flowers wilt, I'll get tired of the plant and regret buying it.

The source of my frustration is the orchid's blooming cycle. The flowering period for a phalaenopsis orchid can last up to three months. The longevity of each flower is impressive, but after that, the plant is done blooming for a whole year. In effect, I have to carefully tend to the plant all year long, but it will only bloom for a few short weeks. Even the leaves barely grow during the dormant period. Typically, before an entire year passes, I'll get tired of the plant and throw it away or forget about it and let it die.

In the fall of 2021, my patience finally outpaced my neglect with orchids. Earlier in the year, someone had given me several orchids as a gift. Once they were done blooming, I considered throwing them away, but instead dumped them unceremoniously together into one pot. Orchids aren't actually planted in soil, so I threw several handfuls of mulch and old leaves on them. I could have bought orchid growing media, but

I wasn't invested enough to spend any money on the orchids. Finally, I sat them in a deeply shady area outside and ignored them.

The orchids thrived in the rain, heat, and humidity. Since they looked so happy and healthy, I brought them into the house when the weather cooled. I still didn't give them much thought or attention, though, and plopped them on the floor beside some larger plants.

A few weeks later, however, I noticed new growth emerging from the orchids. Now fully invested, I anxiously watched as they continued to grow and promoted them to a place on the table. The stalks elongated and buds began to emerge. Eventually, the buds opened into stunning purple flowers that everyone in our home enjoyed.

My orchids are a reminder that patience bears beautiful fruit. Look at what the Psalmist says about patience.

> *I waited patiently for the Lord to help me,*
> *and he turned to me and heard my cry.*
> *He lifted me out of the pit of despair,*
> *out of the mud and the mire.*
> *He set my feet on solid ground*
> *and steadied me as I walked along.*
> *He has given me a new song to sing,*
> *a hymn of praise to our God.*
> *Many will see what he has done and be amazed.*
> *They will put their trust in the Lord.*
>
> ### *Psalm 40:1–3*

The Psalmist was well aware that God blesses patience. Moreover, he tells us that when other people see the fruit of our patience, they are blessed as well! Just as everyone in my home enjoyed my orchids, everyone you love will be blessed by your patience.

Patience isn't an easy virtue to cultivate. It's even a little scary to pray for patience, because God often provides hard situations to hone our skills. Yet, our most difficult struggles often reap the best rewards. Let's pray for patience today and get ready for God's beautiful blessings!

Lord, thank you for providing me with opportunities to grow in patience. Please forgive me for getting impatient when you don't act as quickly as I desire. Help me grow in peace and faith during my seasons of waiting on you. I look forward to your future blessings, both in my own life and in the lives of other people who will see your hand at work. In Jesus' name, Amen.

Personal Reflection

Spend a few minutes in prayer asking God to help you grow in patience. If you are currently struggling with any situations in which you need God to move, confess your faith that God will provide exactly what you need to bear fruit at the right time.

_____

_____

_____

_____

_____

_____

_____

Day 80

New Direction

Yesterday I talked about my orchids blooming. I didn't mention the setback during the process. When the first stalk had grown to about six inches long, something broke it completely off. I don't know what happened. I simply walked by one day and saw the broken stalk lying on the floor. Most likely, the orchid had an encounter with a dog or teenage boy, but we'll never know.

I was beyond disappointed. I thought that my chance at getting orchid blooms was over. Little did I know that more stalks would grow. Even better, the broken stalk grew back. It simply made a right turn and started growing in a different direction.

I think the broken orchid provides a meaningful lesson. Sometimes we feel devastated by a loss, an ending, or an unexpected change, when God is simply taking us in a different direction. According to Proverbs 16:9, "We can make our plans, but the Lord determines our steps." In other words, don't hold your plans too tightly because God might take you in a different direction. Maybe a relationship ended that you thought would last forever. Maybe you lost a job that you loved. Maybe your business failed, even though you gave your best effort. Maybe you didn't get into the college that you wanted. Maybe you were shocked, shattered, and broken, but God wasn't. The turn of events that came as a complete surprise to you did not take God unaware.

You and I have limited knowledge and narrow vision. Our Lord sees the past, present, and future, and his power extends to all creation.

Furthermore, "The faithful love of the Lord never ends! His mercies never cease," (Lamentations 3:22). Many things in our lives will end, but God's love and mercy are eternal. If something in your life has ended, if your heart is broken, or if your effort simply wasn't enough, God has something better prepared for you. He can create new growth out of what was broken and turn your disappointment into joy. As Samuel said to the children of Israel, watch and see the great things the Lord will do (1 Samuel 12:16)!

Lord, thank you for your unceasing love and mercy. Thank you for determining my steps even when I don't notice your guiding hand. Forgive me for doubting your goodness when I've been disappointed in the past. Help me to view endings through the eyes of faith instead of fear. Help me to live with joy and peace in my heart, even when life takes unexpected turns. In Jesus' name, Amen.

Personal Reflection

What disappointments or unexpected life situations are you facing? Instead of viewing your circumstance as a failure, ending, or defeat, consider it the beginning of something new. Make a list of opportunities and blessings that can emerge from your new direction.

_____

_____

_____

_____

_____

Day 80

Day 81
Feeble Faith

Yesterday we talked about the unexpected turns life can take. Sometimes the course of life simply doesn't go as you expect. Rest assured though, God has good plans and future blessings as long as you continue to trust him and remain on his path.

When the people of Israel exposed their feeble faith by asking for a human king, God remained faithful. The Lord answered their request by appointing King Saul and as a bonus, sent rain for their crops. When the people of Israel acknowledged God's hand at work, Samuel reminded them, "Be sure to fear the Lord and faithfully serve him. Think of all the wonderful things he has done for you," (1 Samuel 12:24).

Over and over, Samuel exhorted Israel to remain faithful to God. He knew that the Israelites were prone to waywardness, and sure enough, a short time later King Saul exposed his own feeble faith. Saul got tired of waiting for Samuel, disobeyed God, adopted the role of a priest, and offered illicit sacrifices. When Samuel arrived, he gave Saul a scathing rebuke.

> *"How foolish!" Samuel exclaimed. "You have not kept the command the Lord your God gave you. Had you kept it, the Lord would have established your kingdom over Israel forever. But now your kingdom must end, for the Lord has sought out a man after his own heart. The Lord has already appointed him to be the*

leader of his people, because you have not kept the Lord's command."

1 Samuel 13:13–14

Instead of walking in God's plan and trusting in God's timing, Saul bulldozed his own path. As a result, he removed himself from God's provision and protection. Although God wanted to bless Saul with a prosperous kingdom and a lasting legacy, Saul chose his own path—an excruciating spiral into jealousy, rage, and paranoia.

Like the people of Israel, you and I are prone to go our own way. When God doesn't move quickly enough or when life takes a surprising turn, we often race toward the quickest or easiest solution. However, Proverbs 14:12 warns, "There is a path before each person that seems right, but it ends in death." Because our knowledge is limited and our foresight is dim, we can't see the dangers ahead. But God's plan leads to life and blessing. He knows the future and protects us as we follow him. Let's learn from the forebearers of our faith and heed the words of Samuel: "Be sure to fear the Lord and faithfully serve him. Think of all the wonderful things he has done for you," (1 Samuel 12:24).

Lord, thank you for all the wonderful things you have done in my life and for the blessings you have prepared for my future. Help me to live in reverence and faith so that I'm not tempted to step outside of your plans. Give me the patience to wait on your timing and the self-discipline to obey you, even when a quicker or easier solution seems available. Give me clarity and discernment to make wise decisions and healthy choices. In Jesus' name, Amen.

Personal Reflection

Meditate on any decisions, disappointments, or unexpected situations you are facing. Are you making decisions based on expediency or faith? Are you tempted to take the quickest and easiest path or are you waiting on God's wisdom and timing? Pray over each situation, confess your faith in God's plan, and ask him to guide you. Spend some time in prayer and meditation, and write down anything you feel the Lord might be saying to you.

_____

_____

_____

_____

_____

_____

_____

_____

_____

_____

_____

_____

_____

_____

Day 82
A Sunny Disposition

The holiday season can be a time of loneliness, depression, and anxiety for many people. Statistics vary, but up to 20% of people claim that the holidays have a negative impact on their mental health. In our post-covid era, mental health continues to decline dramatically, especially during the holidays. Why are rates of depression higher than normal during the holidays and what can we do about it? We'll discuss this topic more over the next several days, but today let's start with the basics.

Seasonal and physiological factors can have a major impact on mental health. During the fall and winter, the weather is colder, and the days are shorter. As a result, many people tend to stay inside more and exercise less. If that describes you, get up and go outside! Even low-intensity exercise stimulates the release of endorphins, which increase feelings of happiness and reduce stress. Exercise also helps regulate circadian rhythms, which facilitates better sleep. In fact, as little as 30 minutes of exercise several times a week has an impact on mood similar to taking an antidepressant medication.

If you go outdoors for exercise, the benefits of your workout are exponential. Sunlight stimulates the release of serotonin, which triggers feelings of peace and happiness. Exposure to sunlight also helps balance melatonin, which works in tandem with serotonin to help you stay alert during the day and sleep soundly at night. Sunlight also stimulates the production of vitamin D, which improves mood and boosts the immune system.

Taking a simple step like going outside for a walk can have a profound impact on your mood. Although sunlight and exercise won't fix all your problems, they may trigger the motivation to take further steps toward health and happiness. According to Proverbs, "A cheerful heart is good medicine, but a broken spirit saps a person's strength," (Proverbs 17:22). On the other hand, depression is a downward spiral that saps our strength and steals our joy.

The enemy wants to steal, kill, and destroy your health. He knows that "the joy of the Lord is your strength," (Nehemiah 8:10), so he'll do everything he can to keep you down. If you are at rock bottom, he will try to keep you there. If you are on top of the world, he'll try to knock you down. Wherever you are, God has provided an endless supply of joy and strength. Sometimes, we just need to take one step in his direction. Today, that step might be a literal step outside your door!

Lord, thank you for giving me a joyful heart, a peaceful mind, and a strong body. Thank you for providing joy that is not based on circumstances and strength that the enemy cannot steal. Help me make wise choices that foster mental health and physical wellness. Give me the discipline to make time in my schedule to steward my physical body so that I can serve you effectively. As I live in joy, give me opportunities to share the source of my joy, you Son, Jesus. In Jesus' name, Amen.

Personal Reflection

If exercise isn't part of your regular routine, take some time now to schedule it into your calendar. Start with a realistic goal, like a 15-minute walk three times a week. Then, make some time today to get a quick workout, spend some time outside, or both!

Day 82

Day 83
So Happy Together

Yesterday we talked about the loneliness, depression, and anxiety that many people experience during the holidays. Today, we'll continue exploring two questions that I posed: Why are rates of depression higher during the holidays and what steps can we take to fight the trend? As we discussed yesterday, two tools with which we can fight depression are physical activity and sunlight. However, the causes of depression run much deeper than being cooped up inside, and the solutions are much more complex.

In an earlier devotional, we talked about communal behaviors. Many species of animals thrive because their community, pack, flock, or herd works together for survival. Earlier humans also banded together into tribes. Our survival literally depended on it. Humans aren't the strongest or most resilient creatures on the planet. Although we are the smartest, we lack many skills that give animals an advantage. We don't have sharp teeth or claws. We can't climb trees very well or run very fast. As humans, our strength has always come from working together.

Although modern technology has connected the world in unprecedented ways, we are more isolated than ever. Covid quarantines made our isolation even worse, but they actually exposed a problem that already existed. Each of us live in our own separate bubble. Even when we are physically together, we exist in separate digital worlds on phones, tablets, and computers.

Our isolation causes problems because community is an essential human need. If any of our essential needs are not met, we operate in deficiency mode. In deficiency mode, mental health, fulfillment, and growth are nearly impossible.

In case you missed it, let me emphasize that our fundamental human needs can only be fulfilled in the context of relationships. If you are struggling with depression or anxiety, you aren't broken, you are simply a human with unmet needs. If you'll allow him, God "will supply all your needs from his glorious riches, which have been given to us in Christ Jesus," (Philippians 4:19).

Friends are often the avenue through which God meets our needs. According to Proverbs 17:17, friends "are born to help in time[s] of need." That's why the enemy will try to keep you isolated from friends, overwhelmed with work, and afraid of rejection. However, Satan is the father of lies, and you serve the God of truth (John 8:31–58)! Today, let the truth of God reign in your mind and allow him to meet your needs.

Lord, thank you for meeting every need in my life. Thank you for provision, protection, and people. Help me to be intentional about cultivating relationships. Help me make time for meaningful relationships and fun social interactions. Help me view people that come across my path as avenues of blessing in my life. Forgive me for instances in which I've viewed other people as annoyances or distractions. Allow me to see people through your eyes and love them with your heart. Allow me to be the means by which you meet the needs of others in my life. In Jesus' name, Amen.

Personal Reflection

Reach out and spend some time talking to a friend today. Set a date to get together for lunch, dinner, prayer, or a fun social activity.

Day 84

Lament or Languish

The last couple of days, we talked about the loneliness, depression, and anxiety that many people experience during the holidays. So far, we've discussed three tools that can help ward against winter woes: physical activity, sunlight, and community. Today we'll continue adding to our toolbox with a strategy that may be surprising to you—lament.

In general, a lament is a passionate expression of sorrow. In the biblical context, however, a lament is often accompanied by an expression of hope in God's rescue or intervention. Many laments of David are recorded in the book of Psalms. In Psalm 42, David cries:

"O God my rock," I cry,
"Why have you forgotten me?
Why must I wander around in grief,
oppressed by my enemies?"
Their taunts break my bones.
They scoff, "Where is this God of yours?"
Why am I discouraged?
Why is my heart so sad?
I will put my hope in God!
I will praise him again—
my Savior and my God!
Psalm 42:9–11

Through lament, David models a transparent intimacy with God. He confesses honest thoughts and emotions. He feels like God has abandoned him, he feels ridiculed and rejected, he feels purposeless and alone. David doesn't offer stale platitudes or stock prayers; he lays bare the contents of his heart before God.

Lament can be a powerful part of the healing process as long as it doesn't deteriorate into languishing. When we lament, we express our heart-felt sorrows to God and confess our trust in his care. When we languish, we wallow in our sorrows and blame others, including God, for our problems. When we lament, we get on with life, even if we don't feel like it. When we languish, we make sure everyone knows how miserable we are. When we lament, our attention is fixed on God. When we languish, our attention is fixed on our problems. Instead of seeking growth and healing, those who languish seek every opportunity to advertise old wounds and rehash past hurts. Ultimately, languishing is toxic to the mind, soul, and body.

On the other hand, lamenting offers mental, emotional, and physical benefits. The act of crying actually releases endorphins into the bloodstream. Further, studies have shown that tears activate the parasympathetic nervous system, which turns off the fight or flight response and soothes the body into a state of rest. Articulating our sorrows also helps detoxify the brain, increasing cognitive function and decreasing the risk of neurodegenerative diseases like Alzheimer's.

In reality, God already knows our deepest thoughts and most desperate struggles. Lament simply helps us acknowledge what God already knows. Lament can even be considered a form of praise because in bringing our sorrow to God, we acknowledge his power to help. As we cry out, we are reassured within the strong arms of our Father.

Lord, thank you for your abiding presence throughout my seasons of joy and my seasons of sorrow. Teach me to bring my cares to you with transparency and honesty. Help me to trust you even when my emotions tell me that you don't care. Help me keep my eyes fixed on you rather than my sorrows. Thank you for moving on my behalf even when I don't see your hand or feel your presence. In Jesus' name, Amen.

Personal Reflection

Read Psalms 42–43 and notice how David feels about himself, God, and other people. You may want to write down a few thoughts about what you can learn from David's honesty. If you feel the need, practice your own lament before you complete your quiet time for today.

Scan the QR code for passages of Scripture

_____

_____

_____

_____

_____

_____

Day 85
Giving and Guano

For several days now, we've been talking about strategies for overcoming the loneliness, depression, and anxiety that many people experience during the holidays, or any other season, for that matter. So far, we've discussed four tools with which we can fight depression: physical activity, sunlight, community, and lament. Each of these tools requires us to take proactive steps to put them into practice. Today we'll look at another proactive strategy—service.

Emotional struggles sometimes arise when we feel purposeless or unappreciated. Hopeless and anxious feelings will continue to grow as long as our attention remains on self. When we focus too much on ourselves, our needs and problems appear larger and larger until they are all that we can see. Yet, our needs can only be filled by our Father, and our purpose can come only from him.

Every living creature is invested with purpose by the Creator. Let's consider bats, for example. Not many people appreciate the important role that bats fulfill. Most notably, bats function as living, breathing insect repellant. They protect you and I from mosquitos and protect our crops from other invasive pests. They eat literally pounds of mosquitos and other insects per day. Upon digesting the pests, bats then promote crop health by spreading fertilizer. Their waste, guano, is one of the best fertilizers in the world.

If strange little creatures like bats serve a purpose in this world, you most certainly do. Each of us has a distinct purpose, yet we also share a common purpose—serving one another. Although the principle runs contrary to logic, we are most fulfilled when we sacrifice our own desires to serve God and his people. According to Proverbs, "The generous will prosper; those who refresh others will themselves be refreshed," (Proverbs 11:25).

As we increasingly deny self and serve others, our own joy and fulfillment grow proportionately. Luke explains, "Give, and you will receive. Your gift will return to you in full-pressed down, shaken together to make room for more, running over, and poured into your lap. The amount you give will determine the amount you get back," (Luke 6:38). Luke isn't referring only to financial generosity. When we give grace, we receive grace. When we give love, we receive love. When we give kindness and offer forgiveness, Jesus promises a life of abundance and fulfillment.

Our gracious Savior and our loving Father know that when we serve and sacrifice for others, we create room to receive. Because we aren't clinging so tightly to our things, our hands are open to receive from God. Let's offer our lives to the Lord, follow in the steps of our savior, and serve God's people. Your life may not transform overnight, but when you wait expectantly and serve faithfully, you'll soon experience fulfillment and joy beyond your wildest expectations.

Lord, thank you for giving my life purpose and fulfillment beyond measure. Help me to serve selflessly rather than focusing on my own desires. Give me the motivation to serve even when I don't feel like it. Open my eyes to opportunities and needs around me. Show me how I can meet the practical needs of those in my life and my community. Help me also to give more encouragement, grace, love, and forgiveness so that I can experience a closer intimacy with my Savior as I become more like him. In Jesus' name, Amen.

Personal Reflection

Instead of focusing on your own needs and wants today, be attentive to the needs of others. Be intentional about offering encouragement and kindness, as well as helping others in practical ways.

_____

_____

_____

_____

_____

_____

_____

_____

_____

_____

_____

_____

_____

Day 86
Vision Therapy

For a few days now, we've been discussing tools for overcoming the loneliness, depression, and anxiety that many people experience during the winter. The five strategies in our toolbox so far are physical activity, sunlight, community, lament, and service. Each of these tools requires us to take proactive steps to put them into practice. Today we'll look at one more strategy that requires action—Bible study.

Research indicates that Scripture engagement is directly proportional to human flourishing. In other words, individuals who regularly study and read the Bible tend to have higher levels of joy and fulfillment. Scripture is the primary means by which we receive hope, learn about our Lord, and discover how to live out our faith. The Psalmist teaches, "Your word is a lamp to guide my feet and a light for my path," (Psalm 119:105).

Unfortunately, many of us struggle to understand Scripture or simply find it boring. Bible reading feels like a chore, so it gets shunted to the bottom of our priority list. If you feel this way, you're not alone. You simply haven't discovered the right tools. Let me illustrate with a personal example.

When Abel was in his first few years of school, learning to read was a massive struggle. Even worse, the struggle translated into every subject since reading is a fundamental skill for learning just about anything. Finally, after years of struggle, one of Abel's teachers asked some key questions and helped Abel articulate why reading was so difficult for him. According to Abel, "the words moved around on the page." In reality, we discovered that Abel's eyes were, in fact, moving around. He was soon diagnosed with nystagmus, a condition in which the eyes jitter and jump uncontrollably.

To correct the issue, we began attending vision therapy twice a week. The vision therapy itself was excruciating, but the homework was even worse. For 30-60 minutes every afternoon, Abel and I had to complete complicated visual puzzles and writing exercises. We had to partner for odd vision tracking activities that required swinging a ball vertically, horizontally, and in circles. Finally, after two torturous years of vision therapy Abel's vision and reading skills were impeccable.

I share Abel's struggle to highlight the fact that there may be reasons why reading your Bible is daunting. I'm not implying you need vision therapy, but you might need to explore different resources to facilitate growth. Perhaps you need to find a translation of the Bible that is easier to understand. Perhaps you are an auditory learner and need to *listen* to the Bible instead of reading it. Perhaps you need to find a book or take a course that teaches you to read and study effectively. Perhaps you need to identify a study guide that will clarify how the multitude of people, places, and events in the Bible fit together.

Like vision therapy, the earlier stages of the process can be challenging. You may need to exercise firm self-discipline to develop your spiritual muscles. Even as your skills grow and you become a more proficient student of the Bible, you'll always have room to grow. The Bible is so rich and compelling that we can spend our entire lives mastering its truths. But as we immerse ourselves in God's Word, he simultaneously gives us a hunger for more. What strategy are you going to sample today?

Lord, thank you for providing your Word as a lamp to my feet and a light to my path. Give me an abiding desire to immerse myself in

Scripture. Lead me to the tools that will help me learn effectively and grow continually. As I study, give me understanding through the power of your Holy Spirit. Teach me to receive your instructions with gladness and apply them in my life. As I seek you through your Word, grow my wisdom, faith, and joy. In Jesus' name, Amen.

Personal Reflection

Prayerfully evaluate your own habits of Bible reading and Bible study. Ask God to reveal one step you can take to grow in your knowledge, skills, or discipline. You may want to consider one of the tools I suggested or identify a different strategy that is appealing to you.

_____

_____

_____

_____

_____

_____

_____

_____

_____

_____

_____

Day 87

Our Spiritual Alphabet

For almost a week, we've been discussing strategies for overcoming the loneliness, depression, and anxiety that many people experience during the winter. Yesterday, we talked about Bible study, which is a strategy for overcoming mental and emotional struggles, but also a practice that is key to living a flourishing, abundant life. Research indicates individuals who regularly study and read the Bible tend to have higher levels of hope, joy, and fulfillment.

Today, I want to bring your attention to a passage of the Bible that highlights the value of Scripture. Psalm 119, the longest chapter in the Bible, is presented in the form of an acrostic. Each section of the Psalm begins with a letter of the Hebrew alphabet. We could even say that Psalm 119 is the alphabet for our spiritual life.

You'll be better served by reading Psalm 119 for yourself than by reading my words about it. Therefore, I'll keep my own words brief to provide you more time to read the psalm for yourself! But first, let's pray.

Lord, thank you for your Word, which provides joy, protection, and guidance for my life. Give me the desire and discipline to study your Word daily. Help me to continually grow in my knowledge of you and my understanding of salvation history. Guide me as I seek to live out the principles I learn so that I can bring glory to you and grow your Kingdom. As I grow in knowledge, help me also grow in purity, love, forgiveness, faithfulness, and grace. In Jesus' name, Amen.

Personal Reflection

Read Psalm 119. If you have time, read the Psalm a second time and write down everything you learn about God, about those who follow God's teaching, and about God's Word, instruction, and law.

Scan the QR code for passages of Scripture

_____

_____

_____

_____

_____

_____

_____

_____

_____

_____

_____

Day 88
Lucille the Bearcat

For roughly the last week, we've been talking about strategies for overcoming the loneliness, depression, and anxiety that many people experience during the holidays, or during any other season. So far, we've discussed six tools with which we can fight depression: physical activity, sunlight, community, lament, service, and Bible study. Each of these tools requires us to take proactive steps to reap their benefits. Today we'll look at one final strategy, one which requires restraint— eliminating comparison. In other words, we must be proactive *not* to compare ourselves with others.

To illustrate my point, I'd like to tell you about Lucille the bearcat. Lucille is Rico's neighbor at the Cincinnati Zoo. If you recall, Rico is the Brazilian porcupine we talked about last month. Rico and Lucille have much in common. Both animals live in trees; each boasts a prehensile tail and dexterous claws that help them navigate their habitat. Both Rico and Lucille are animal ambassadors for the zoo, which means they often leave their enclosures for encounters with guests, visits to schools, appearances on television, and other fun educational activities.

If I'm honest, I think most people would prefer a visit from Lucille. Her fur is soft and snuggly, unlike Rico's sharp quills. Lucille smells like buttery popcorn, as opposed to onions and body odor. Most notably, Lucille is even the mascot for the University of

Cincinnati. She regularly makes appearances at basketball, baseball, and football games.

Can you imagine if Rico compared himself to Lucille? He might become jealous of her soft fur and appealing scent. Rico might envy Lucille's trips to ballgames. He could begin to resent the fun times Lucille has with friends and fans. Instead of enjoying his own life, Rico might begin to feel depressed, insignificant, and unappreciated. Instead of happily eating peanut butter in his tree, he might sit in the corner and sulk.

It seems silly that Rico might compare himself to Lucille. Why would her happiness diminish his own? Rico probably wouldn't even enjoy the ballgames. Lucille is curious and energetic, and she doesn't mind the crowds and loud noises that would terrify placid little Rico. Both Rico and Lucille are uniquely designed and especially suited to their individual lives.

Comparison is the enemy of contentment. We often feel jealous when we hear about the accomplishments of others or see the highlights of their lives on social media. Scripture teaches, however, that we shouldn't measure our worth in comparison to others.

Comparison and jealousy are fundamentally rooted in pride. We subconsciously think we deserve better than others and we want what they have. Paul teaches, "Don't be selfish; don't try to impress others. Be humble, thinking of others as better than yourselves," (Philippians 2:3). In a different epistle he warns, "Don't think you are better than you really are. Be honest in your evaluation of yourselves, measuring yourselves by the faith God has given us," (Romans 12:3).

Our self-worth should be based only upon God's standards and our identity as his children. When our contentment comes from him, our confidence can't be shaken. Our joy isn't diminished by the successes of others. In fact, if we celebrate the blessings of others, our joy will only grow. When we let go of comparison, we take our eyes off the blessings of others so that we can see the multitude of blessings in our own life!

Lord, thank you for your abundant grace in my life. Help me to take my gaze off of the blessings of others so that I can appreciate your favor over my own life. Forgive me for pride, selfishness, and covetousness. Give me joy rather than jealousy at the gifts and successes of others. Teach me to live in humility and be more like my Savior. In Jesus' name, Amen.

Personal Reflection

Be conscious of the tendency toward comparison today. Make a mental note of situations in which you are tempted to feel resentment or jealousy. If you use social media, be especially self-aware of your thoughts and feelings while you peruse stories and posts. Whenever you find yourself in a state of comparison, try to shift your mindset to one of celebration and gratitude.

Day 89
Waiting by the Window

Smokey's favorite place in the entire house is Asher's bed. From his perch on the bed, he can access the window, where he will shove the blinds out of the way with his nose and press his face against the glass. Sometimes Pepper joins Smokey for guard duty, but most of the time she prefers to nap.

From his vantage point at the window, Smokey can see our driveway, our street, any dog-walkers, and all passing cars. What he loves most, though, is to greet us when we arrive at home. As we pull into the driveway, we can see his whole body start to wiggle and wag. He then disappears from the window so he can greet us immediately at the door.

Sometimes I wonder if I am waiting and watching for Jesus as diligently as Smokey watches our driveway. Numerous passages of Scripture admonish us to stay alert and prepared for Christ's return. I appreciate 1 Thessalonians 5, in particular, because Paul provides more detailed instructions than usual. First, he teaches, "let us be sober, putting on faith and love as a breastplate, and the hope of salvation as a helmet," (1 Thessalonians 5:8). When we wear faith and love as a breastplate, we fill our heart with so much faith and love that no hurtful emotions can penetrate. Rejection, unforgiveness, bitterness, and hate have no ground in which to take root. When we wear salvation as a helmet, we guard our thoughts against lies of the enemy. The truth of Christ and the certainty of our salvation protects us from deception and doubt.

Second, Paul instructs us to support each other. In 1 Thessalonians 5:11, he says, "Therefore encourage one another and build each other up, just as in fact you are doing." Paul exhorts each of us to be part of a healthy faith community. When we encourage one another, we strengthen each other's faith and help each other walk in God's plan. Living out faith in isolation places us in a vulnerable position, and God desires to keep us safe and strong!

My heart fills with happiness when I see Smokey's face in our window. Although he is just a dog, I'm inspired and encouraged by his devotion to our family. When you and I prepare for Christ's return with love, faith, and hope, we encourage every person in our faith family. We foster expectancy and excitement that strengthens our bonds in Christ and moves the Gospel message forward.

Ask yourself if you are going to lay down for a nap like Pepper or watch at the window like Smokey. Your Savior is coming soon!

Lord, thank you for your incarnation on Earth, which helps us understand the Kingdom of God. I look forward to the day you return to establish your Kingdom for eternity. Help me be diligent to prepare myself and encourage those around me. Help me to be so full of faith, hope, and love, that no scheme of the enemy can gain purchase in my heart. Help me faithfully encourage and strengthen my brothers and sisters in Christ. Give me a passion for spreading the Gospel so that all people come to know you. In Jesus' name, Amen.

Personal Reflection

Prayerfully read 1 Thessalonians 5:1–11. Ask Jesus to show you how you can take one step to be more prepared for his return today.

Scan the QR code for passages of Scripture

Day 90
Only the Beginning!

When I was a little girl, my favorite book series was *The Chronicles of Narnia*, by C. S. Lewis. I read each of the books at least six times, and some of them more. I was so obsessed with Narnia, that I searched for an entrance behind every door and inside every closet. I longed to experience Narnia with an intensity that brought tears to my eyes.

I didn't realize at the time, but in his series of children's books, C.S. Lewis presented deep truths about our faith. The story of Narnia was, in fact, the story of salvation. My longing for a Savior who was both gentle and fierce eventually brought me to the feet of Christ. My resolve to fight on the side of goodness and love led me toward the path of ministry. My desire to learn more about a Kingdom of faith, hope, and love spurred me into more than a decade of seminary learning. Even as my childhood obsession with Narnia came to an end, my journey of faith was only beginning.

I've followed Christ for nearly 25 years now, and I'm still getting started. Even when this life ends, the next one will begin. In the light of eternity with Jesus, the closing lines of *The Chronicles of Narnia* still make me cry.

> *And for us this is the end of all the stories, and we can most truly say that they lived happily ever after. But for them it was only the beginning of the real story. All their life in this world and all their*

adventures in Narnia had only been the cover and the title page: now at last they were beginning Chapter One of the Great Story which no one on earth has read: which goes on forever: in which every chapter is better than the one before.

Every season eventually ends, but each ending brings opportunities for a new beginning. Wherever you are in your faith journey, I pray that you are expectant about the future. I pray that the concepts you've learned through our time together will propel you into your next season with joy. Seasons will end, but faith, hope, and love remain forever (1 Corinthians 13:13). May you cling to God's love so fiercely that each chapter is even better than the one before!

Lord, thank you for providing faith, hope, and love to sustain me through every season of life. Give me the endurance to make the most of every season of life and every opportunity that you place before me. Help me to grow in perseverance and fortitude so that I remain faithful even during the difficult seasons of life. Show me what you would have me learn in every stage of life. Guide me as I seek to serve you faithfully and share your love with others. In Jesus' name, Amen.

Personal Reflection

Prayerfully meditate on the last several months of devotionals. You may even want to flip backward through the pages and read some of the notes you have written. Take extra time today (perhaps tomorrow as well) to celebrate growth and identify next steps. Organize your thoughts into three lists and write your notes below. First, celebrate areas in which you have flourished over the last 90 days. In what areas of life have you become more healthy, mature, and established in your faith? Second, identify areas in which you are currently growing. What strategies are you implementing in order to become healthier? What habits or patterns of thought are you allowing God to prune from your life? Third, identify a few opportunities for future growth. What seeds can you plant today in order to produce healthy fruit in future seasons of your life?

_____

_____

_____

_____

_____

_____

_____

_____

_____

_____

_____

_____

_____

_____

CPSIA information can be obtained
at www.ICGtesting.com
Printed in the USA
LVHW111457310822
727298LV00005B/259